CALLED TO
SPEAK
LEAD &
IMPACT

CALLED

TO

SPEAK LEAD & IMPACT

20+ EXPERTS SHARE WISDOM AND LESSONS ON LIFE & BUSINESS

WENDI BLUM & PATRICIA WOOSTER

WoosterMedia

TABLE OF CONTENTS

INTRODUCTION

A Personal Message

Welcome, new friend, to *Called to Speak, Lead, and Impact*. You arrived here at the right time. We are humbled and honored you have chosen to be here with us.

We want to take a moment and express what's in our hearts. It's simple. Our intent is to leave a legacy of goodness in the world. That's it. *You* are the reason why we wrote this book. You matter. You deserve to live a beautiful and prosperous life. Truly, we all do.

As you prepare to dive into the pages ahead, we suspect there might be something stirring inside of you that says, "You are meant for something more." You may or may not know what it is. Perhaps you are changing careers or embarking into the world of entrepreneurship for the very first time. Or maybe you've started thinking about the dreams you put on hold awhile back and are willing to re-explore again.

On the other side of the coin, maybe life has been a struggle for you, and you have been drawn here to find a way to go from victim to victorious, from being stuck to discovering a breakthrough, or from feeling like an imposter to owning your power and stepping into your new empowered identity.

Regardless, we don't take any of these considerations lightly. Wherever you are on life's journey, we want you to know you are not alone. By being here, you'll discover new insights and ways to unleash your heroism, talents, masterful work, and future identity as well as methodologies to boost your business, grow your income, and expand your personal freedom.

Before we move forward, we want to pause here and acknowledge who you already are. You are a bright beacon of light in the world with genius, divine gifts, and unique talents inside of you that the world needs now more than ever. Really take that in. Now is the time to narrow the gap from fear to faith, scarcity to abundance, and from worry to freedom.

Understanding this book has been a process, like all of life, which has been energizing, exhausting, exciting, and immensely rewarding. Each one of our 22 coauthors came together as a collective, co-creating for the greatest and highest good of all. All had a big mission in their hearts and a burning desire to make a positive impact on the world. It's been a deep journey individually and as a whole, going well beyond our comfort zones. On the other side, we've become better human beings in the process.

As you read on, you will experience the vulnerabilities, real life experiences, and passion of each one of the authors that came together to produce this thought-provoking and masterful body of work. Each one has a calling and an undeniable desire to leave a positive mark in some way, shape, or form on the world.

It is our heartfelt wish for you to step into the next bountiful season of your life with an awakened vigor and newly acquired knowledge as you tap into your zone of genius and create your own masterful work.

Wendi
Together we are stronger, better, and wiser.

HOW CAN I DO GOOD AND CREATE SOMETHING MEANINGFUL THAT LASTS LONGER THAN I DO?

Wendi Blum Weiss

CHAPTER 1

ANSWERING THE CALL BY WENDI BLUM WEISS

When I was forty-five years old, I had a big aha moment. I was working out at the gym, kicking around ideas with my personal trainer trying to come up with something cool to create that I could turn into a side business.

I started working at a very young age. In high school I made donuts and served coffee at the local donut shop. To put myself through college, I worked almost full-time at Publix for four years while taking a full curriculum at Florida State University.

After I graduated, many of my classmates were moving to Atlanta, and I thought that would be a great place to start my career. So off I went and got my Series 7 and went right to work as a financial planner for E.F. Hutton. After a year, I decided I wanted a career change and went on to have three different jobs over the next five years. All were sales related at Pitney Bowes, Dictaphone, and Panasonic. The whole time I kept a side hustle to make some extra cash.

Always ambitious and seeking opportunities, my roommate and I started a company called Wall of Distinction. We did high-end wallpapering and custom painting in some of Atlanta's most beautiful homes. We worked on weekends, and it was a great source of additional revenue.

I worked for two Fortune 500 companies: Pitney Bowes and Dictaphone. Both were excellent companies with superb sales training programs. There I was in my early twenties selling copy machines to brick-and-mortar businesses and recording devices to doctors. Sales became my jam. Go figure!

One of my all-time favorite sayings by Steve Jobs is "You can't connect the dots looking forward; you can only connect them looking backwards." I'll discuss this in more detail later.

The recording devices I sold to doctors from Dictaphone totally intrigued me. It was the '80s. Medical doctors would carry the device in the pocket of their white lab coat and verbally record the findings after seeing each patient. Thank God there was a system in place to capture the information since we've all heard the jokes about the sloppy handwriting of most doctors. At the end of the day, doctors would turn in the cassette tape (yes, I know it's crazy how far we have come) to a transcriber who would type the notes for them.

I started keeping my own Dictaphone in my car to capture my personal notes after seeing my accounts. Moreover, from time to time, I would use that same recorder to record what I was thinking about. I will come back to this point later.

Then along came fax machines, and I was one of the first to leap into what I saw as a lucrative, growing business. I was in the right place at the right time until I wasn't. I had a three-state territory and made great bonuses. However, the industry faded away about the same time I was having my first son, Daniel. I knew I wanted to stay home for the first year anyway and was confident I would find another growing industry to jump into when I was ready to go back to work.

As luck would have it, I met a woman while the two of us were playing with our babies in the neighborhood pool. She told me she loved being a pharmaceutical representative because it was a great income with flexible hours. Bingo! I found my next opportunity. Not knowing a lot about that industry, I researched all the major companies and called for applications. I filled out a number of them and I accepted a job with AstraZeneca. I was very happy there for five years, but then my entire life changed, and I became a single mom of two.

The Big Pharma companies divided up their sales department into two divisions:

1. Primary Care, consisting of thousands of representatives, calling on most doctors, family medicine, internal medicine, etc.
2. Specialist: a much smaller salesforce that is highly specialized in one disease state.

I worked at the primary care side at AstraZeneca.

When Bristol Myers Squibb reached out and asked me to interview with them, I wasn't actively looking to change companies. After giving me a list of reasons why I should consider them—no samples which meant no inventory, a smaller list of doctors, working in their HIV division—it sounded appealing. It was a hot topic in America at the time and on the front page of every newspaper. I wanted to get involved.

They recruited me to educate, advocate, and create outreach for underserved communities. That is when the bells went off. I could roll up my sleeves and work behind the scenes to make a difference in the world. Oh, one last thing. Significantly more income. I was in. This became my home where I stayed for the duration of my pharma career.

As I was doing curls, toning up my biceps, and throwing out ideas with my trainer, I was thinking about the phase of life my kids were in. They were in high school, and I was happily remarried. Things were status quo. Sorta. My career was humming. I had a great track record, worked for and with great people, and made a prosperous living. I won awards, contests, and was given incredible opportunities throughout my tenure there. I was offered many promotions; however, I couldn't accept them because it required relocating or extensive traveling.

All good, right?

Growing up, we struggled. Our single mom worked hard. There were times we barely could get by. I endured hardships. I still have to this day a vivid memory of our mom crying as she counted her tips

7

after her shift at Rosa Maria Pizzeria when she got home at night. My stomach would churn as I would try to ignore it and fall asleep. I couldn't. It haunted me.

Money. It carries a great deal of emotion with it. At least it did in our household, although I suspect it does in many. I myself was willing to work hard and do whatever it took to have enough of it. Lots of hours? I could do it. Need to get the job done? I've got you. Want someone to take the lead? Count me in. I seem to have come into the world wired to work and get things done.

If truth be told, I learned a strong work ethic out of necessity. No one was coming to save me, and I needed to pay some bills.

On paper it looked like I had arrived. I had a college degree, a great career, a beautiful home, two great kids, friends, went out for dinners, and traveled. Yet somehow along the way, I could feel something big was missing. I didn't know what it was at the time, so I covered the feeling up and just lived my life.

For as long as I could remember I had this underlying anxiety. It would consume me. Sometimes I felt like I wanted to die. I would then sweep the emotional unrest under the rug and go back to the constant busyness of my life. Work gave me a sense of purpose. Work gave me a way to push away the pain. I kept it to myself and suffered in silence.

My happy place is the gym. On this particular day my trainer handed me a card that said destiny. It hit me like a lightning bolt. I could design a clothing line around the word "destiny." I got excited that I found my side hustle.

My first stop after leaving the gym was Target. With tee shirts and markers in hand, I couldn't wait to get home to create my first designs. Destiny grew into "What is your destiny?" and it had instant success. The popularity of the sayings was the secret. For example, *My Destiny is to be Strong, Powerful, Courageous, and Fearless.* And so on. With thirty plus sayings in total, the Destiny clothing line blew up. In one week Chelsea Lately wore one of our destiny shirts on her TV show, Rachel Ray wore one on her cooking show, and Whoopi Goldberg introduced it on *The View*. Not only was Destiny a financial success but a spiritual one. Having to read the same 30 sayings over and over again changed my perspective and changed my own life. Within a few years I was a different person. It was the future me I didn't know existed calling me to come create her. And so I did.

I realized what I wrote on a shirt could be spoken out loud and people were yearning for the messages on them. Many of them were just like me, stuck, going through life feeling unworthy, like an imposter, struggling, and maybe even suicidal. They may have felt that something was missing and were searching for something more. It was imperative for me to step up to the plate and share my voice, story, and message.

There were two ways to do it: one to one, which would take enormous time and effort, or one to many, by speaking in front of an audience on stages and through social media. Yikes! Me speaking on stage? No way! I wasn't a public speaker, nor did I want to become one. I had to figure out a way to get over myself. It wasn't about me; it was about impact.

The only thing that got me on that first stage and many more afterwards was focusing on my *big why*. I certainly understood the power of having a mission statement. Bristol Myers Squibb proudly shared theirs at every single one of our big meetings – "Our Mission: To discover, develop and deliver innovative medicines that help patients prevail over serious diseases."

I wrote out two copies of my own mission statement and framed them, keeping one on my nightstand and the other on my office desk:

My mission is to inspire men and women from around the world to tap into their power and unleash their brilliance, voice, and message to make a bigger difference in the world.

There was still another problem yet unresolved. My old self-image hadn't quite caught up to the new one. There was the whole "I'm not good enough" imposter syndrome wired into my identity. Remember back when I worked for Dictaphone? I connected the dots and had another aha moment. I could record my own voice and reverse-engineer myself as a dynamic, engaging, and powerful speaker prior to it actually being true. Scientifically what that means is I could change the biochemistry in my body to catch up to and match my new self-image. I knew I had created my signature system that others could use to upgrade their identity, too. All I wanted to do was share it with as many people as possible.

My first speaking opportunity came while I was taking a coaching certification course, followed by several others and I concluded I had no other choice but to leave Bristol Myers Squibb. It was scary stepping into the unknown to start a new career as a professional speaker, mindset coach, and yes, writer too at the age of 50. Certainty. When you know without a shadow of a doubt it is your calling, you feel the fear and do it anyway. So I did.

My company Success Blueprint was born, and I discovered the answer to my own question. What is your destiny? This was it. Within a year, I had three satellite offices and a full practice. Many of my clients were either coaches or were in corporate and wanted to become a coach. I taught them the dynamics of the REYNI (Reverse-Engineering Your New Identity) the unique framework and signature system I teach as I segued into business consulting specifically for speakers and coaches.

What unique formula, framework, or feature do you offer your community or clients?

Our brains want to preserve energy, which is why we gravitate towards easy-to-follow steps and systems. Over the last 12 years in the coaching world, I have systemized all of my programs and teach my clients, who are also coaches for the most part, how to do the same.

I'd like to offer you my top three.

1. The Seven Success System for Higher Level PPI (productivity, performance, and impact)

   Compass Setting is getting crystal clear from a thirty-thousand-foot perspective of the actualized results you desire most.

Vision Priming is priming the mind to see with vivid detail the outcome before it actually happens to such a degree that you can actually feel it as well.

Activating and Aligning is a daily ritual of aligning with your mission and purpose to induce a flow state.

Going Granular is another important mental conditioning exercise to unleash deep creativity and mastery level results by going deep as opposed to going wide.

Overcoming is the mind shaping routine I use with clients to evoke and build courage, strength, resilience, and power to move beyond limiting beliefs into their unparalleled potential.

Becoming is a methodology I developed to help my clients step into their next level self-image as a speaker, coach, leader, and human being using future scripting and guided imagery.

Conviction is stepping into certainty and the ultimate, knowing that you are called to serve humanity and the world with your message, gifts, unique talent, and personal story.

2. The Stellar 5 for a Positive and Productive Day
   1. Wake up early, ideally at 5:00 am and hydrate
   2. Implement meditation and breathwork
   3. Move the body (work out, walk, stretch, do something that gets the blood flowing)
   4. Write down goals and priorities
   5. Visualize a successful day backwards

3. REYNI (Reverse-Engineering Your New Identity)

   Combining my core philosophy from before, if you can actually see it, believe it, and achieve it, you will integrate your new identity and new story deep enough into your subconscious mind to make it stick. Here is the process broken down.

- **Mission, Vision, Values, and Principles -** Write out the essential four, the key to living one's highest integrity of personal truth.
- **The Hero Within Self-Worth Process** - Speak your self-worth into existence
- **The Seven Success Steps Deployment** - As noted above
- **Your Slay the Dragon Forever Protocol -** Declare war on the self-sabotage syndrome that plagues many
- **Your New Story Download -** Rewrite the narrative of your story, scene by scene, in vivid detail, and out loud with total conviction.
- **Recruitment of Your Senior Advisors -** Gather your role models: guides, heroes, and people you admire most. Trust you are supported
- **The Last Breath Circle of Love -** Go forward in time to your very last breath. See yourself surrounded by the people you love and who love you, an incredible circle of peace and unconditional love. Speak out loud how proud you are of the life you've created, and lastly, how much you fully, deeply, and unconditionally love yourself.

These are just a few. I have also created an entire community of heart-centered, mission-driven leaders to lock arms with you. In this community, the Speakers and Coaches Society (SACS), made up of about twenty thousand members, we also host events, monthly training, and five-day challenges. On a personal note, I offer ways that I work with clients, teams, organizations, or individuals.

1. Private coaching
2. Masterminds
3. Membership

All are available to fast-track your reach, revenue, and impact. When I was exiting the pharmaceutical industry, I knew community was a big part of what I desired going forward. I didn't know of just the right one, so I created it. I hope you will join us.

What role does collaboration have in your current business?

Collaboration is everything. From the day I stepped out of the corporate environment into the world of entrepreneurship, I realized I couldn't do it alone. Hence, I started building community and partnering with strong leaders.

I created three core pillars, community, connection, and collaboration around one central theme: leaders who have a mission-driven message in their heart. Thus, SACS became the central core of our business.

Our philosophy is "Together we are stronger, better, and wiser." We encourage our members to build bridges instead of walls, to consider how much further you can go as a team as opposed to alone, and how much synergy you have when you bring together the collective for the greatest and highest good of all.

How were you able to transform a setback into a setup for success?

I would be remiss if I don't answer this question. Up until I was 45, I was riddled with fear, self-doubt, and low self-esteem. Growing up was tough for me. I had suicidal thoughts and felt like I didn't belong. I hid my feelings because I was ashamed of them, which felt even worse. I was living as a total imposter.

I share my personal story here not for sympathy but with the hope that it helps someone begin to believe in themselves. I am not the greatest, but I am the best. I am the best version I can be, and I will keep getting better because I know I can keep improving. So can you.

What do you want to be remembered for? What is your ultimate legacy?

The first part of my ultimate legacy is to be the best version of myself as a role model for my two sons, grandson, and future generations. It is the single most important consideration in everything I do. I strive to leave my mark on the world by being a loving, present, and insightful parent who raises two men and their offspring to be great human beings.

The second part of my ultimate legacy is my chosen career and line of work as a business consultant and mindset coach for speakers, coaches, leaders, and entrepreneurs. I feel incredibly blessed to have discovered my professional calling, which is directly linked to contribution and impact.

To tie both parts of the legacy equation together, the overarching question I live by is "How can I do good and create something meaningful that lasts longer than I do?" If I can touch one life in a positive way or perhaps a hundred or more, then I have achieved my ultimate, personal, and business goals, a life of meaning and contribution.

How can people connect with you?

I can be found at wendiblum.com and on Instagram @wendiblum.

THERE'S SOMETHING SO FREEING IN BEING ABLE TO ASK FOR HELP OR ADMIT YOU DON'T KNOW.

by Patricia Wooster

CHAPTER 2

GROWTH IS AN INSIDE JOB
BY PATRICIA WOOSTER

There was no such thing as an introvert when I was a kid. A person was either shy or outgoing, and I was labeled as shy. The expectation was for me to be quiet, intelligent, responsible, and easy-going. In reality I was reflective, sensitive, funny, and creative. I wasn't athletic, overly social, or particularly studious. I bounced between two houses every week, one where I felt free to be myself and the other where I needed to be cautious. This made for a confusing childhood and added to a list of insecurities as I entered adulthood.

Luckily, I was a hard-ass worker. I got my first job at Dairy Queen at the age of 14 and never looked back. I have always loved to work. There's something magical about earning your own money and gaining new experiences. And as a kid, it is a great equalizer because all you need to do is show up, work hard, and play nice with others. I have worked at some interesting places from restaurants, timeshare properties, and group homes to selling computers and software. Every single one of those opportunities taught me something new about business and myself.

Throughout my life, the common thread has been writing. I started documenting my life in diaries when I was ten. I wrote poems, letters, and stories. I wrote about my hopes and dreams. I wrote when I was sad, mad, or upset. And as I got older, I wrote for the college paper and graduated with a creative writing and psychology major. No matter where I was working or what I was doing, I always took the time to put pen to paper.

It took me fifteen years to get my first book deal. The fear of losing it kept me from telling my publishers at Simon & Schuster that I was sitting in an emergency room in 2016 with a collapsed lung. It also kept me from telling them about the other eighteen nights I spent in the hospital within a few months following that first event. Every time they sent me an email, whether in a hospital bed or at home recuperating, I promptly answered it. I may have also forgotten to mention a significant lung surgery that resulted in six days in the hospital and a few months when I didn't leave my house. I didn't tell them that the two hours a day I spent creating the teacher common core guide to go with my book were the only hours I spent upright for an entire week. No, I forgot to share that bit of information, but that's the beauty of email.

This is what happens when you get used to living within the shadow of who you really are and believe others bring more to the table than you do. You refuse to ask or admit you need help because you think it exposes a weakness. I lived with this fear for many years. It was an idea that people and opportunities fall within a specific hierarchy, and a person's behavior and actions are dictated based on whether those things are above or below you on that scale.

Since I believed my opportunity with Simon & Schuster was above me, I held on to my secret. The recovery from surgery was long and painful. While the marketing team at the publisher kept adding book launches and promotional events to my calendar, I struggled to walk from my bedroom to the kitchen. I don't recall any of the details of those first two months, but I know that I said yes to every deadline and opportunity they asked of me.

My first scheduled event was four hours away from my home at a high school. An hour into my three-hour workshop, I needed to sit, so I finally opened up and told my health story and some of the difficulties from my childhood. It completely changed the dynamic of the room. Suddenly, the teenagers who had spent the first part of my speech staring at their phones started sharing their stories too. Many of them started following me on social media, and some were still emailing me updates on their lives three years later. This is when I finally understood the power of vulnerability and transparency.

The stories we share, whether through word of mouth, books, or speaking are so powerful because that is how we connect. Many of us grew up in circumstances where there was shame or secrecy, and it is easy to feel alone. This is why the reaction in that high school gymnasium was so intense. As soon as I lowered my veil, it gave them permission to do the same. Maybe one of my experiences was similar or perhaps it was just a shared feeling or emotion, but for one hour, there was healing in that room.

My lung surgery and the events that followed changed the entire trajectory of my life. From the books I read to the people I met, I discovered the only thing that truly matters is *impact*. The very definition of that word is to "create an effect," whether it's on yourself or others. My health journey has taught me the importance of intentionality, priorities, and vulnerability. The fantastic people I continue to meet show me support, grace, and the best of humanity.

I built an entire business around helping as many experts as possible write and publish books that create a massive impact on their audience and business. We've done this by taking everything I've learned from big publishers like Simon & Schuster and bringing those high standards to the self-publishing industry. It's about leveraging someone's earned expertise into a book that takes them from being the best-kept secret to a sought-after expert.

My next opportunity for impact came in 2022 when I met Amilya Antonetti and her vision for impact aligned with the vision of WoosterMedia. As the most sought-after human behaviorist in the world with some of the most innovative expertise and tools, I jumped at the opportunity to work with her. During this process, we discovered we are truly better together, so we started the merger for my company to be part of the Designing Genius brand. We are working together to change the way businesses view human capital and allow people to bring their best genius into their personal and professional life.

This growth in the last couple of years is because I finally owned my seat at the table. I stopped asking for permission and grabbed a chair. All of my experiences and expertise when paired with other people who possess cohesive genius, create the most amazing collaborative and exciting environment. I don't need to have all of the answers or even a majority of them. I just need a piece of the puzzle and the ability to partner with those who contain the others. I wish I had this confidence twenty years ago, but I am so glad I have it now. There's something so freeing in being able to ask for help or admit you don't know. If I can pass this piece of my journey on to my two sons, then it is the best advice I can give.

Where have you been called to lead? What is the *why* behind what you do?

My *why* is to help shine a light on the genius inside of people. Each one of us has something very special about us. It is not about who has the most likes or followers online. Many of the most brilliant people in the world don't have a social media presence, so it is about bringing those people forward for the rest of the world to benefit from that knowledge and history.

Think about what we learn when athletes share their stories. It is much more than about sports. We learn about mental strength, grit, resilience, mindset, fear, and courage. That information and those stories need to be studied so people can learn and grow from them. The ramifications on future generations is to understand that psychological, neurological, and physical components can impact everyone. And that's just one example. This is why TED Talks and documentaries are so important. They bring together people who are thinking about a topic in a new way or are educating people about an underrepresented subject.

I recently met someone who is the last known descendant of a tragedy that resulted in hundreds of people from her community being killed in the early 1900s. No one related to the event has ever publicly spoken or written about it for fear of retaliation. Before her grandmother passed, she gave my acquaintance a detailed account of everything that occurred and asked her to write and share the story. Think about that for just a minute. American history almost lost the details of a massacre that resulted in the loss of hundreds of lives. This important book my friend is writing ties in to a nonprofit and her work to rebuild her community.

Every person I work with is connected to my *why* because they are using what they know or have experienced for the betterment of others. Sometimes they don't understand why they feel called to share what they know or whether anyone will care, and it is my job to help them find out. Together we go searching for where we can create the most significant impact, whether it is writing books, creating digital programs, teaming up with schools, public speaking, or finding corporate or college sponsors.

How were you able to transform a setback into a setup for success?

You can't make money as a writer. Those were the encouraging words I received two weeks after graduating college with a degree in creative writing. It's incredible how fast a person can go from being idealistic and passionate about a career to looking for a safe job that pays the bills. But that's exactly what I did. I absorbed all the expectations, fears, and conservative views of those around me. This is before the internet and online job sites made it easy to apply for jobs worldwide. I only knew about available positions through my Kansas City Star newspaper, and writing was not a hirable category.

My first real job was at a huge call center, where we sold computers in cow-spotted boxes. I spent the following ten years moving from one software sales position to the next until I finally landed in Tampa, Florida. When I became pregnant at age 31, I knew I would not return from maternity leave. Before my son was born, I closed a deal that funded his college account. That was the last time I worked for someone else.

As a stay-at-home parent I decided to write my first book. I did all of the things a person was supposed to do by joining a writer's group, attending conferences, getting a writing partner, and reading up about how to pitch my idea. Once the first draft of my young adult fiction book was complete, I queried agents with no success. The book was actually pretty terrible, so that didn't help.

Instead of giving up or continuing down the road of rejection, I tried something else: building relationships the way I did in my software sales career. A friend of mine who wrote educational work-for-hire books mentioned a shortage of freelance fact-checkers and offered to make some introductions. MediaBistro offered a short certification program, so I signed up and learned the ropes. Within a few months over fifty manuscripts sat in my email inbox from various traditional publishers.

To be clear, factchecking is not a glamorous job. It's hours upon hours of verifying that every single sentence in a nonfiction book is true. It's slow and tedious work for little pay. My computer crashed multiple times from various viruses after visiting hundreds of websites per day. I started using disposable laptops so that I started with a clean slate every year.

While the work wasn't amazing, the contacts were incredible. As a former software executive, I understood the power of networking and relationships. I never missed an opportunity to talk to a publishing editor on the phone or to do a little extra work to be noticed. I kept meticulous notes on every conversation and knew what was happening at each publishing house.

My opportunity came in 2014 when an editor at Simon & Schuster mentioned a new nonfiction series for teens they were contracting out for writing. I raised my hand to be a writer for two of the books. To my surprise they said "Yes" without requiring an agent, writing sample, or jumping through any of the standard hoops. I delivered both of those manuscripts early and without issue.

This opened the door for me to pitch my passion project *Ignite Your Spark,* a nonfiction book for teens based on the research and training of the most innovative leaders in adult personal development education. Over the phone I shared my entire vision of the project with my editor. Without hesitation she told me she loved it and mentored me through the process of creating the book proposal. They published the book in 2017, selling thousands of copies and creating more opportunities than I could have ever imagined. It wasn't until the 13th book that I even needed an agent, which is not only uncommon but unheard of in this industry.

What role does collaboration have in your current business?

Nothing in my current business or life happens without collaboration. Right now, with our company merger, we are building twelve revenue streams within this new business. Every single one of them is in partnership with someone else. The core business unit is set up as a collective to begin with, so it only makes sense to build upon that model. Every single day I get to work not only with my husband, but with other amazing people who have truly chosen community over competition. We do not bring our ego to the table but operate from a place of the greater good of the company.

When I started my journey into entrepreneurship, I believed there was something very noble about building the business alone. I spent years doing it this way and was very wrong. Working within a silo closes you off to new ideas and makes it very difficult to see the gaps in your thinking and ideas. It removes the innovation that comes when you bring different people together who have genius in various areas. Right now I am being stretched in new ways because I am mind-melding with other people who share my interests but have different skill sets and knowledge. It's much more exciting and rewarding to build something as a collective.

Think about it this way, how much time in a day do you have to strategize, do the work, deliver the product, and build your business?

Now, add on networking, social media, administration, personal development, and marketing. This is impossible for one person to do. Even with a virtual assistant it is a very hard business model to scale quickly.

Don't get me wrong. I did it for years, but it kept me out of my zone of genius 80 percent of the time. Because I was juggling all of the different departments of my business, I had less time to devote to the area where I really shined. This became abundantly clear when Amilya and I started working together and I felt a runner's high every time we collaborated. Our projects immediately threw me into a flow state because they perfectly aligned with my genius. My performance and growth in those areas have skyrocketed very quickly because it is a perfect fit for me. This is why collaboration and community are so important in entrepreneurship. We can all find that flow state that pushes us into that runner's high, where we perform at our highest level. Imagine the job satisfaction and success employees would have if they could tap into that state every time they worked?

What do you want to be remembered for?
What is your ultimate legacy?

My ultimate legacy comes back to the word *impact*. The first layer of that impact starts at home with my sons. Every single thing I do has them at the core, from what projects I choose to take on to how I address conversations some parents may avoid. I give more thought and care to the men they will become than anything else because I know that is the biggest impact I can have on this world.

Outside of my family, my ultimate legacy circles back to how I earn a living. I want to be remembered as someone who helped bring voices to life that people need to hear. It is more than just storytelling but creating tools and resources that expand people's thinking. I want to help people heal and bring them together. Those are the projects that incrementally affect change in generations moving forward. Every time we improve something in this world, regardless of how small, it multiplies and impacts every single person who comes next.

It is like how scientists describe the butterfly effect, where the flap of a butterfly's wings may ultimately cause a tornado. If I can play a small part in the process, I feel my legacy is complete.

The greatest reward in these legacy goals is that I am building them with my husband, Scot. We have intentionally put our sons and their futures as our driving force. And just last summer, Scot exited corporate America to join me in business so that we may build our professional legacy together.

How can people connect with you?

I can be found at woostermediabooks.com and on Instagram @ PatriciaWooster.

IT TAKES IMMENSE
COURAGE TO FOLLOW
YOUR HEART,
BUT WHEN YOU'RE
GIVEN THE OPPORTUNITY,
DON'T LOOK BACK.

by Bianca Abbott

CHAPTER 3

EMBODYING TRUE WELLNESS
BY BIANCA ABBOTT

My quest for healing began when I was eight years old after discovering that my mother received HIV-tainted blood while giving birth to my younger sister, Charla. This was the catalyst for me to travel the world and step into my power as a modern-day medicine woman. My journey led me to study and work with the world's most prominent healers, doctors, yogis, and shamans.

My mother's diagnosis caused deep trauma and anxiety for my family and me. Growing up in the '80s and '90s, very little was known about this disease — how it could get contracted or prevented. As a result, we lived in fear of the stigma and being ostracized from the community. So we kept it a secret to protect my family. However, this secret made us sick.

It took a toll on my father's mental health, leading to crippling addiction and an accidental overdose of prescribed opioids. I was 20 years old and heartbroken. I never thought I would lose my father before my mother. I always thought he would be there by my side to deal with life's challenges.

His death was catastrophic but also the catalyst for my mission to help others overcome trauma and chronic health conditions. I was determined to figure out how to transform this karma and alchemize it into my dharma, my life purpose.

Due to this stress, I was diagnosed with chronic pain and fatigue, migraines, irritable bowel syndrome (IBS), temporomandibular joint (TMJ), obsessive-compulsive disorder (OCD), anxiety, depression, post-traumatic stress disorder (PTSD), attention deficit hyperactive disorder (ADHD), and an autoimmune condition. Within my family alone, we had an alphabet soup of diagnoses impacting our physical, mental, and spiritual well-being. It was clear we were not getting the help we desperately needed.

After a lifetime of trauma and excruciating pain, I dedicated my life to finding the best healing modalities in the world. First, I committed my studies to Western medicine. I wanted to be a psychiatrist at the time, so I studied psychology at Eckerd College. Then I entered a post-bacc pre-med program at Columbia University and studied for the MCAT to become a doctor. After seeing a psychiatric nurse practitioner for my anxiety and depression, I was inspired to pursue this career path instead. I earned a bachelor's degree in nursing at NYU and a masters in nursing at the University of Miami.

For many years, I truly believed in the power of Western medicine. Still, it became clear through my healing journey and my family's health experiences that it wasn't a holistic solution to our ailments. We needed something that could heal us at the root and transform our health. After over a decade of taking synthetic drugs, seeing my mother and sister suffer, and not finding relief, I decided enough was enough. I made a plan to get my family off pharmaceutical drugs and devoted myself to natural healing.

Then eight years ago, I went through the dark night of my soul. My worst nightmare was becoming a reality. My mother was near death, and I was on my knees for a miracle. In the darkness, a light came on. Every morning for 40 days, my sister and I took my mother to 4:00 a.m. Kundalini Aquarian Sadhana in Miami, Fl., and something truly miraculous happened. In the healing vibration of this ancient yogic practice, my mother came back to life!

It took five years of intensive therapy for her to recover and come back into her essence. During that time, I studied with master healers like Dr. Sebi, Dr. Morse, and Alexander Cousins, who are helping people heal from so-called incurable diseases, like cancer and HIV. I traveled to India and Bali and immersed myself in fasting, Ayurveda, psychedelics, alkaline veganism, and kundalini yoga. **With my guidance, my mother defied all odds, became medication-free, and the HIV virus is undetectable in her blood after 38 years.**

My journey has not been an easy one. It took me years to find the secret to thriving health, and now it's my duty and honor to spread this knowledge. By combining fasting, alkaline vegan nutrition, herbs, Ayurveda, psychedelics, and kundalini yoga with self-discipline, self-love, and perseverance, I was able to bring myself and my family back to health!

Through the culmination of my experiences, I learned that the current system does not work. We need a new system for healing mental, physical, and spiritual illnesses. We are in the midst of a global health crisis, and it's time to look beyond the stigmas and utilize ancient time-tested healing modalities combined with modern-day medicine to improve the health of humanity.

What is the *why* behind what you do?

I serve as a bridge between Eastern and Western medicine and empower my clients to heal at the root and embody. My mother's diagnosis of HIV, my father's passing, and my own health challenges were the turning points for me to dig deep into the rabbit hole of natural healing and immune restoration. Diseases impact entire families, and my family was no different as we all suffered from various degrees of depression, anxiety, and trauma. What I discovered was that Western medicine covers up the symptoms like a Band-Aid on a wound. It was never meant to be curative.

Fortunately, Eastern medicine is extremely effective. It is a travesty that this information and education are not readily available to the general public. When you keep the cures from society a secret, it shows how deeply sick our healthcare system is. I believe that everyone has a right to this information to achieve health sovereignty.

From the age of fourteen, I knew that Western medicine wasn't the only solution, but I needed a traditional education to introduce this information in a way that people could trust me as an expert. I committed my life to my studies and learning from the top experts in the world. At the same time, I've been a dedicated yogi for the past 24 years. I'm on my mat either leading 4:30 a.m. community Sadhana or for my individual practice. It's foundational to my success and healing, but I also wear a white coat and work in the clinic, facilitating ketamine therapy. This is how I master both worlds. The yogi hosts retreats in India, Nepal, and Bhutan. The white coat practitioner sees patients in the office and consults with physicians and leads psychedelic journeys at Mercy Hospital in Miami, Fl. Finally, the two worlds are bridging together! As a fifth-generation nurse and the first nurse practitioner in my family, I blend the two philosophies and the two environments so I can meet patients where they feel most comfortable.

"The natural healing force within each of us is
the greatest force in getting well."
—Hippocrates

This is why I do what I do. I've healed myself and empowered my family, community, and thousands of people around the world to step into their superpower.

What unique formula, framework, or feature do you offer to your community or clients?

My unique formula comes from a global understanding of healthcare. I studied at some of the best schools in America and worked at some of the top hospitals in the world. Since the age of 16, I traveled the globe doing humanitarian, missionary, and clinical work with Indigenous tribes, children, refugees, and families. Getting exposed to different cultures challenged my perspective of what true medicine is. I discovered that the healthiest people are the ones who cultivate fresh water from the rivers, eat from their gardens, honor their families, and are aligned with their mind, body, and soul. Some of my favorite cultures include Bali, India, Nepal, Myanmar, Uganda, and Costa Rica. I spent years living, breathing, and connecting with other cultures so I could bring this wisdom back to America.

Through all of my experiences, I realized how disconnected Americans are from nature, fresh organic food sources, clean water, self-love, and overall wellness. Despite having a holistic upbringing with nutrition and seeing my mother use food as her medicine, I didn't discover how far removed Americans were from their true health until I studied with Dr. Sebi and Dr. Morse, who helped heal people from all diseases. From their teachings, I learned how critical regular detoxification and cellular rejuvenation are for our bodies so that we eliminate and release the toxins, mucoid plaque, parasites, candida overgrowth, and balance out the microbiome to properly absorb essential nutrients. Our gut health is vital to thriving health for all systems. When we destroy our gut, we destroy our first protection from pathogenic microbes and toxins found in our foods and environment. As Hippocrates says, "All disease begins in the gut." I realized that Western medicine was diagnosing people based on toxic symptoms and not focusing on the main culprit of dis-ease. This led me to create the LunaFast.

The LunaFast is a 10-day holistic wellness and fasting program that combines ancient detoxification practices with modern science to activate and empower the healer within. Instead of traveling to India or Bali, you can do this virtual program from the comfort of your home. Over the course of three years, I have guided over a thousand people around the world to cleanse and heal themselves.

Every month on the new moon, we fast in community. We set our intentions and get clear on our wellness goals. We offer a 70-page fasting bible complete with an alkaline vegan elimination diet, self-love rituals, herbal and gut cleansing protocols, and much more. Last year, we produced the LunaBox, which is our detox in a box with all the tools you'll need for a powerful transformation shipped to your front door. Some benefits of our program include fat loss, mental clarity, glowing skin, reduced acid mucus inflammation, vital energy, etc. We recommend cleansing on a seasonal basis to maintain thriving health and decrease the risks of chronic and mental health conditions.

This past year my business expanded, and I took the leap of faith in leading the psychedelic healing movement. Psychedelics have been integral in my family and community for alchemizing deep-rooted familial and ancestral trauma. I spent the last eight years sitting with the top shamans and diving deep into this mystical world. Currently, psychedelic medicine is misunderstood, and the stigma still lingers within the general public. For instance, when you hear the word psychedelics, maybe the first thing you think of is illegal drugs, danger, or drug addiction. This is the picture that has been painted for you by the media, Big Pharma companies, and the government. Although psychedelics used recreationally can be dangerous, when they're used intentionally with a trained health care provider or shaman, they can be life-changing. The psychedelic revolution is happening now! We can't stop this movement because it is deeply shifting our world and opening doors to an ancient collective practice of healing.

I currently see clients at Spine and Wellness of America in Miami, FL. for ketamine therapy and integration. Ketamine is a class lll dissociative anesthetic psychedelic that was approved in 2019 for treatment-resistant depression, anxiety, depression, brain injuries, and cancer.

"I began ketamine therapy and integration with Bianca when I was at the lowest emotional point in my life. The ketamine was a game changer in that it gave me a perspective that is inaccessible in normal states. It returns your nervous system to ground zero, and it makes you understand that you are an important part of a larger whole." —Hester Esquenazi, 2022

Ketamine therapy is extremely effective when done with integration. The brain is in a state of neuroplasticity and is ideal for doing ancient practices to reprogram the subconscious mind. Psychedelic medicine opens your mind, while integration allows you to explore it. I include the following in my integration sessions to ensure a powerful transformation:

1. Kundalini yoga
2. Meditation
3. Breathwork
4. Sound healing
5. Nutrition and herbal protocol
6. Shadow work, inner child work, and trauma therapy
7. LunaFast: Detoxification and cellular rejuvenation

Through my journey of working with clients over the past 10 years and creating programs for powerful transformation, I opened the door to Quantum Healing Medicine. This combines mind-body medicine merging Eastern and Western practices and is based on the universal consciousness theory. You may be familiar with one of the leading experts, Deepak Chopra. Essentially, I empower my clients to use their innate life force energy to heal themselves by shifting their energy at a quantum (or subatomic) level. It is my mission and passion to provide this personalized medicine for the evolution of global consciousness.

How have you pivoted, shifted, or expanded in your business in the last few years?

The defining moment in my life was truly a divine intervention. I had to go through a major breakdown to have a breakthrough. After enduring a tremendous heartbreak and betrayal, I fell to my knees in desperation. At first, I sought healing from Mother Ayahuasca in the jungles of Costa Rica. However, I didn't realize the level of trauma that I was confronting, and ayahuasca pushed me over the edge. I was scared to be alone and was in a crisis, and that's when ketamine therapy fell into my lap.

I had my first ketamine session a year and a half ago, and it allowed me to calm my nervous system, release the fear, and rise like a phoenix. At that point, my belief system around Western medicine changed. I realized that not all synthetic medicines are created equal, and ketamine, when used intentionally, is a gateway medicine for the psychedelic healing movement. Soon after this life-changing experience, leading experts of ketamine therapy in Miami reached out to see if I was interested in joining their team. Looking back, everything was in divine alignment. Once I took the leap of faith, trusted the process, and fully surrendered, everything perfectly aligned.

Although I received powerful healing, I still wanted to see firsthand in clinical practice the power of this medicine. After witnessing overwhelming positive results and miracles in the last year, I decided to make this a mainstay in my practice and step fully into my role as a psychedelic nurse practitioner.

What life or business lessons have created the most growth for you?

Having a strong spiritual foundation is key to being a successful entrepreneur. My spiritual practice is my saving grace. It's allowed me to navigate the darkest times with love, compassion, and forgiveness. When I'm in alignment with my mind, body, and spirit, I'm able to magnetize the clients, relationships, opportunities, and abundance to get to the next level. I have learned that when I give the reins to my higher power, everything falls into place more perfectly than I could've imagined. At the end of the day, it takes a lot of consistent hard work to be an entrepreneur. There's no quick way to success. But when you are following your divine dharmic path, you have an innate life force fiercely guiding you.

Having great mentors, business coaches, healers, and therapists have been essential to me being at the top of my industry. I stay in my lane and receive guidance and support when it's outside of my expertise. That's why I attracted a team of rockstars to empower me to expand my vision, realize my blind spots, and keep me accountable. Having a support system that inspires me and puts the fire underneath me to rise is one of the greatest blessings. When you rise together, magic happens.

Specializing in a niche, seeing the trends before they happen, and being a pioneer in the industry have been integral to my success. It takes immense courage to follow your heart, but when you're given the opportunity, don't look back. Simply fly and trust that you have all of the tools to be successful.

What do you want to be remembered for? What is your ultimate legacy?

As someone with over 10,000 hours of expertise in yoga, detoxification and fasting, medicine, and psychedelics, I want to be remembered as a fearless leader on a mission to guide millions of people on their path. I'm here to show people the natural way of empowering the inner physician and saying no to a sick-care system that is surface-level treatment.

Through my vulnerability, strength, and courage, I want to inspire and educate people to live their best lives. My goal is to break through the stigmas around holistic and psychedelic medicines and change outdated systems so we can get out of this global health crisis. It's my dream to see a world where we embrace the wisdom of nature and connect to our truth. I envision a world where we have clean water right from the spring, gardens where we nourish ourselves, and systems that promote life. We must merge Eastern, Indigenous, and Western technologies to manifest a world of prosperity.

How can people connect with you?

I can be found at lunafast.com and on Instagram @biancaabbottwellness.

I WANTED TO HELP INDIVIDUALS AND ENTREPRENEURS LIKE YOU GO FROM PANIC TO PASSIVE INCOME AND HAVE SOME FUN GETTING HEALTHY.

by Kathy Binner

CHAPTER 4

DESIGN YOUR PATH TO FREESTYLE LIVING BY KATHY BINNER

I was sitting at the red light, saying a little prayer that the gas gauge would not suddenly register empty and that the engine would not sputter and choke to a stop. "Turn green, turn green," I said. Not only was I almost out of gas, but I was going to be late to clock in. The gas gauge pointer was just above the big E. I didn't have time the night before to get gas; working two jobs was exhausting, and it felt like this schedule was killing me or at least destroying my physical and mental health. The only thing that kept me going was payday when the amounts on the two checks added together would pay the rent, the utilities, and the groceries.

Don't get me wrong; I liked my two jobs well enough. One was in the office at an insurance agency, and one was at the front desk of a local hotel checking in guests, hoping for promotion into hotel management. I liked helping people, and I liked the other staff. It was just too many hours, but I didn't know how to stop. After all, I needed the money. I had no health insurance and was living payday to payday with no extra cash for emergencies. I had a car I couldn't keep running, and even worse, I had no means to save towards retirement! But working hard was a virtue, wasn't it?

As I sat at the red light, I saw a young mom pushing her child in a stroller in the park on my right. An older man was sitting on the park bench reading the paper, and a gal was speeding by on her bike. Who were these people? Didn't they have jobs? How did they have the time or the money to walk in the park during everyone's work day, to sit on a bench and not have a care in the world, to read the paper like the day is all their own, and to ride bikes on the beautiful bike paths that wind through the wooded park? Some folks were just lucky, I thought.

I would love to be riding my bike. As a kid growing up out in the countryside, my friends and I would leave right after breakfast and ride our bikes on the country roads until dusk. The rule was when the car's headlights started coming on, it was time to be home. But now I barely had time to sleep, shower, grab a bite, and get clocked in. Sometimes I would wake up and try to remember what job I was supposed to be dressing for. And often I would drive too fast and on empty, just to clock in on time. There was no time to stop for gas. I was a single mom and needed to get home to sleep. Bike riding wasn't even on the list.

I felt guilty being away from my daughter for so many hours. But what could I do? I knew I needed to change my lifestyle or at least my work schedule. I deserved time to take care of my little home, cook a meal, and stop and get groceries or gas. But I told myself it wasn't in the cards for me to have a life like that. After all, I hadn't even gone to college. My high school guidance counselor told me I wasn't college material, even though I had made honor society because our family didn't have the income to pay for my tuition.

My mom had been a factory worker making minimum wage, and my dad had been deemed disabled after severe back surgery before I was born. My mom had an eight-grade education, and my dad had a ninth-grade education. They were so proud that I even graduated from high school, and college was never talked about in our house as I was growing up.

My mom had always supported our family with her meager minimum wage income. My dad had experience in the building trades but didn't or couldn't work for most of my growing up years. Now they both were older and living on social security benefits.

Then something happened that changed my life forever. My mom sat me down and had a talk with me about getting on with it, meaning figuring out a way to make more money. I was crushed! Didn't she see how hard I was working? Didn't she see the hours I was putting in on these two jobs? She was even expecting me to work less! I had just received my promotion into management at the hotel. There was no way I could work fewer hours. I sat alone with these thoughts feeling frustrated and exhausted. How could I make that kind of change? What could I do?

I did take time to get acrylic nails done every two weeks at a local salon, even though I sometimes had to count out my pennies to pay for the service. Nice nails were a part of my "work uniform," so to speak because my hands were signing applications in the insurance office or checking in guests as I worked behind the front hotel desk.

I was quick to think only about myself as my long-time nail tech told me she was retiring after her husband passed away. "Oh, I'm so sorry to hear about your husband," I said as I thought about who I should go to now. I didn't have time to find another nail tech in the next two weeks. She referred me to this young 19-year-old, fresh out of nail school. Humph... I felt very put out that I had to change, and my schedule didn't allow for changes like this. I did feel bad about her losing her husband, though.

I don't know why I thought I could ask my new nail tech how much money she made doing acrylic nails... maybe because she was younger than me or perhaps because she didn't have a college degree or maybe because I was feeling desperate to make a change. But I did ask her, thinking how nice it would be to just sit behind a nail table, eat bonbons, and wait for the next manicure client to arrive.

When she told me she was making more income in one week than I made in a month from my two corporate jobs, I decided to attend cosmetology school, fondly called nail school and become a part-time nail tech. I didn't know if I could make the same amount as her, but what I could make doing nails part-time would satisfy my mom. After all, I could open a small savings account and save a few dollars for my retirement from this side-gig.

At the time, I had no idea the impact this would have. I quit the insurance office job, but I was now working a full-time 50-hour week at my hotel management job and a part-time 10-hour week as a nail tech. I still had no time for my daughter because I was always working or racing from one job to the other. But working 60 hours a week was much better than working 80 hours a week!

How were you able to transform a setback into a setup for success?

When I thought things would improve, the nail salon I signed on with decided to close. My 50-hour-a-week hotel management position was changing into a mandatory bachelor's degree required job, but I had no time to return to school for my bachelor's degree. What was I going to do now?

I was on the downward slide because the nail salon owners decided it was too much work for them to continue operating a salon with kids of their own at home, so they put the salon up for sale. The owners of the corporate hotel were hoping to sell and retire, and the new big corporate hotel buyer wanted all management-level employees to have a bachelor's degree.

I felt panicked! How could I support myself and my daughter without these two jobs? I started researching local colleges to get started on a bachelor's degree as soon as possible to try and keep my corporate hotel job. I started visiting nail salons to find a new salon close enough to my old one so my clients would follow me. Why had I quit the insurance office job? Why had I decided to be a nail tech? What was I thinking?

That's when I truly hit rock bottom. I showed up for work at the nail salon, and it was locked with a big for sale sign in the window. The salon had closed! The next day I showed up for my corporate hotel job, and my boss told me I needed to work more hours. My mandatory 50-plus hours a week was not enough for the new owners. I was extremely exhausted from the uncertainty, the stress, the commute, and the work hours.

I panicked and started looking for a third job. Did I think I could work three jobs? My mom was exhausted from caring for my dad, who had just been diagnosed with pancreatic cancer. My mom watched my daughter who had ADHD while I was racing between jobs, working too many hours, and trying to figure out what to do.

That's when I decided I needed to go full-time as a nail tech since the income was better than my corporate hotel job, even though I hadn't found a new salon yet. I was shocked to discover that I was making more working part-time doing acrylic nails than what my full-time corporate hotel job was paying.

Calculating my nail tech income, I decided I could buy my first home all by myself... a condo. With my nail tech income, I could also afford health insurance for myself and my daughter. So with much consternation and anxiety, I made the leap and left my corporate hotel job behind and went full-time into the salon industry as a nail tech.

Then something happened that changed everything. I found a new salon where the owners had nail techs, hair stylists, and tanning beds. I realized the owners were collecting rent from the other independent contractors and me, but they were paying rent for a storefront in a large shopping center. It occurred to me that I could buy my building, rent it out to nail techs and hair stylists, and add tanning. I could use the rental income to make my mortgage payments, and in 20 years, my staff would buy me a building. My client services would provide for my immediate income needs, and the rental income from a paid-for building would provide for my retirement income needs.

That was the spark I needed! I was scared but optimistic about getting a commercial loan for my very own salon building, and I knew I was on the right path. Here's what happened next. I learned everything I could about the salon industry. I made two additional mortgage payments each year to pay off the building earlier than the 20-year note.

Then one day, I looked up and realized I could now buy four more salon buildings by leveraging my equity and sign on even more stylists and nail techs to pay rent to me, which I could use to pay off these mortgages. I also bought single-family rentals to help grow my portfolio and increase my passive and retirement income.

What life or business lessons have created the most growth for you?

I was forever changed because I now had passive income and the freedom to live the lifestyle I always wanted. I could work fewer hours and even homeschool my daughter for her four years of high school. I started on a new healthy lifestyle.

I now saw myself in control, confident, and a good provider for the first time! I saw myself as a business owner. Much to my surprise, I received the Chamber of Commerce Business of the Year Award and then I received the Chamber of Commerce Entrepreneur of the Year Award.

That's why I couldn't stop. I realized I needed to teach others how to do what I had done. I needed to make getting healthy and creating passive income easier for others. How?

I wanted to help individuals and entrepreneurs like you go from panic to passive income and have some fun getting healthy.

This made me feel like there's so much more for me to do. I was just getting started!

Where have you been called to lead? What is the *why* behind what you do?

When asked what surprised him about humanity the most, the Dalai Lama replied, "Man. Because he sacrifices his health to make money. Then he sacrifices money to recuperate his health. And then he is so anxious about the future that he does not enjoy the present; the result being that he does not live in the present or the future; he lives as if he is never going to die, and then dies having never really lived."

This quote rocked my world! I decided I wanted to give back to the 24/7 workers, the two job workers, the no college education workers, the no trained skills workers, and the single mom and dad workers. You know, folks just like me, and well, the *me* that started this journey.

It was breaking my heart to see would-be entrepreneurs and would-be side hustlers with amazing skills choose to stay in toxic jobs, with mandatory hours that affect their health. They seem to lack confidence, and they seem to have a fear of leaving the security of the corporate world. They struggle with finding the time or the money to create and invest in a side hustle that could grow into a full-time gig to be financially independent. They also struggle to find the thing they feel passionate about.

I believe having additional streams of income is crucial. Sometimes an additional $200–$500 a month makes a huge difference. These amounts can make a difference in having a decent car or having quality daycare. It also breaks my heart that the children suffer the most when the parents can't meet their financial obligations. That is why I decided to develop my online academy with a price point low enough for those who need the information the most.

The current official poverty rate is 10.5 percent, based on the US Census Bureau's estimates. An estimated 39.7 million Americans live in poverty, according to the official measure. As stated by the most recent supplemental poverty measure, the poverty rate is 9.1 percent.

Individuals also transition into and out of poverty over time, though many poor people at any given time will spend multiple spells in poverty. Research shows that transitions into or out of poverty often happen after significant life events, such as marriage, divorce, or sudden changes in income. These transitions also can be associated with more significant shifts in unemployment or wages.

This was me when I started. Just a glimmer above the poverty level. I wanted to create an online academy because I believed the inspiration, the tools and the tribe should be easier than ever with today's user-friendly technology. I wanted folks to choose to change how they think, how they work, and how they play. They might even choose to change their zip code!

For me, it all started with the concept of having total freedom—having passive income and the ability to set the pace of my daily calendar and the overall direction of my life. I was done racing between two jobs and being at the mercy of corporate owners and managers.

I was very motivated by the fact that I could decide for myself. A corporate job didn't fit my sense of independence and wanderlust anymore, so I did everything possible to create my financial security and well-being with passive income and better health habits.

However, the definition of total freedom has changed for me. I learned early on that I didn't just want freedom for the sake of freedom; I wanted to do something with this newfound freedom. I wanted to create things, challenge myself, and value exploring, growth, and learning.

From the work I've now done over the past few years, I've learned I'm not alone in this quest for creative independence and total freedom. More than anything else, most people attracted to these ideas want their definition of freedom. They want the ability to make their own choices and determine how they live. In many cases, they will choose to value this freedom over money, material possessions, or even the perceived security of a traditional profession. The desire for total freedom is what takes someone from a comfortable life to a life of uncertainty but with much more fulfillment.

If you have never experienced total freedom before, it's an exciting discovery. You wake up and go through the day without obligations or expectations. You can choose your adventure, and if you don't like the morning's adventure, you can choose another one in the afternoon.

Most of us want the freedom to be creative and make something meaningful. Our freedom allows us to move towards a higher mission and purpose. So if you're trying to create more freedom for yourself, I think you should ask yourself the following questions: What happens when you get it? What happens after that?

I want to be free with a goal, a project, a vision to pursue. Freedom is the opportunity to choose our own future, but we must choose.

I decided to focus on creating a step-by-step process for others to discover what is their next best step in getting healthy and creating passive income to have this total freedom. I'm focused on creating an even more user-friendly website and launching my online international academy.

What unique formula, framework, or feature do you offer to your community or clients?

My system of teaching and coaching bridges the gap between information, education, and practice by offering ongoing support, which is lacking in many programs. My unique formula is as follows: Practical Education + Informed Practice + Support = Success Information and education are worthless until you put them into practice and priceless when you do. Here are the steps:

- **Step# 1:** Choose a Meetup Group – Do you need to get healthy, want to network more, want to learn how to invest in real estate, or write to create passive income? Join other like-minded folks. These meetups are free and meet often. Choose as many as you would like.
- **Step# 2:** Schedule Your Free Strategy Session – Get Coached – 30 minutes of pure strategy to help you grow and achieve your next best step to freestyle living.
- **Step# 3:** Your Next Best Step Course(s) – Choose your course(s) – Narrow your choices and choose a course that best fits with your goals. Don't forget, your course(s) will be included for *free* in your mastermind group(s).
- **Step# 4:** Simply Start Mastermind Group(s) – Join one of the mastermind groups – In these paid membership mastermind groups, participants raise the bar by challenging each other to create and implement goals and brainstorm ideas. Don't forget, your course(s) will be included for *free* in your mastermind group(s).
- **Step# 5:** Private Individual Coaching Sessions – Individual coaching sessions help mirror your true self, allow you to be

unjudged by others, and enable you to see yourself as you are. It frees you from the desires of others and helps you figure out where you'd like to go and know what you'd like to do. Private individual coaching sessions put you on the fast track to achieving your dreams.

And finally, we offer in-person tribe trips to celebrate your newfound freedom. In today's tech-obsessed world, social media may well be the perfect platform to showcase the world's beauty to armchair travelers across the globe, but travel is so much more than just getting that perfect Instagram shot. Travel should be meaningful. It should excite and inspire you, rejuvenate and ground you, educate and challenge you, and most importantly, humble you.

Travel gives us our greatest stories, our most cherished memories, and countless irreplaceable learnings that we can choose to pay forward to others. It teaches us about ourselves and each other. It broadens our horizons, and just like a reset button, it forces us to refocus on what really matters.

What I'd like you to take away from all this is that no matter how tough things are, keep going, never stop learning, and simply start to find your next best step to getting healthy, growing your passive income, and finally enjoying freestyle living.

What do you want to be remembered for? What is your ultimate legacy?

I want to be remembered as somebody who made a positive difference in the lives of others. I have been a teacher, facilitator, mentor, and coach for years. There are many benefits to the job, and there are a lot of heartaches, more heartache than I care to admit or was prepared for. It breaks my heart when clients decide they can't change their circumstances.

Of all the benefits, the things that mean the most to me are the little things, like when I get an unexpected hug from a client, or when out of the blue, a client says they love my content or programs. Or when I receive a random Facebook message from someone I barely remember, who tells me that I am the only reason he kept pushing forward to become a better person. When a former client decides to become a coach and mentions that I was a motivating factor or that he/she is going to model his/her programs after mine. Those are the things that keep me coming back year after year.

I would like to believe that there are more stories like the ones mentioned above that I am not even aware of. Some stories never get told, but these are the things that remind me why I do what I do for a living, and why I keep showing up filled up every day.

I am currently writing an eBook series, *While I Sleep*, where I share my own financial journey from being a single mom, working two jobs, to retiring early with passive income. As a labor of love, I own and operate the Carraway Guest House B&B, a residential guest house welcoming guests from around the world who walk through my living room.

To give back and serve my clients, I am writing my Simply Start courses, facilitating my online masterminds, conducting my private coaching sessions, and creating the amazing tribe trips. I am helping all who wish to connect, discover a better healthier lifestyle and a passive income option so that they too can take the next best step to creating a healthy lifestyle and passive income.

And that girl on the bike… today that's me!

How can people connect with you?

I can be found at kathybinner.com and on Instagram @kathybinner

THE UPS GUY WAS AMAZED AT ALL THE BOXES I WAS SHIPPING OUT OF MY TINY APARTMENT AND ASKED IF HE COULD BUY STOCK IN MY COMPANY.

by Jeffrey L. Bittner

CHAPTER 5

WHAT COULD YOU ACHIEVE IF YOU JUST ASK? BY JEFFREY L. BITTNER

I was 11 years old when we moved from California to Oklahoma. My dad was a grading contractor who built the Turner Dam in Valley Center, California, commercial shopping centers in Mission Viejo, and freeways among other projects. He had a lot of Caterpillar tractors.

When the energy crisis came in the '70s, he took his tractors and moved us to Oklahoma to strip mine coal. That's where you scrape the dirt off until you reach the coal seam. He had two partners who had the mining lease.

It was a whole new world for me. I would go out to the mine and shoot snakes on the banks of the Illinois River. I had to be careful, though. One day, I was about to step on a poisonous water moccasin when the foreman grabbed me just in time.

My Dad Was My First Mentor

While I was getting my bearings in my new surroundings, my father was growing his business well. He had finally saved up his first $100,000 in the bank when things took a drastic turn. His two partners flew to Las Vegas and lost all the capital on the craps tables.

It broke my dad financially. He could not make his tractor payments and had to give them back. Watching him swallow his pride and do what was necessary to provide for his family was a powerful learning experience. It took him five years, but he taught himself the oil business and started by selling oil leases. Later, he worked in the drilling and production of oil and gas. He would use investors until he earned enough to buy and or drill his oil wells. My dad eventually built an oil business even after losing everything. It taught me to never give up.

At 15 I was grading dirt on a tractor in the scorching heat while dust covered everything. It was a large property, and we were cutting roads to old, abandoned oil wells deep in the woods. We couldn't reactivate a well without roads. One of the early investors came out of California to view one of the oil fields.

Do you want to know the difference between an investor and the guy who makes it happen? The investor drives up with his family in his air-conditioned car. He barely cracks the window open to talk to my dad. He never gets out of his car and drives away. Whereas my dad is the one who negotiated the deals with the lease owners, organized the drilling, hired and managed the contractors, and developed the procedures to complete a well.

My dad had special techniques for doing business with the lease owners. When trying to acquire an oil lease from a land owner, my father would slowly lay hundred-dollar bills out on a table. If the land owner was on the fence, my dad would slowly scoop the hundred-dollar bills back into the briefcase. They would quickly feel the fear of missing out and close the deal shortly after that. My father was the one who got things done. He never stopped at just enough, and he went the extra mile to deliver results.

My dad was my mentor; he wanted to get me interested in the business. Even if I would rather have been riding bikes, he brought me along to business meetings to show me the ropes. He even gave me small overrides on oil and gas wells. For a decade after I left, I would get small monthly payments of about $100 to $170. There is nothing like getting a check in the mail every month. It helped teach me the value of business and what it means to build one.

My dad was pretty hard to work for. I'd get a list of 20 things to do in the morning, and he would grill me about the list when I got home in the evening. There would always be one thing not done, and he would say that was the most important. It did teach me to have a strong work ethic early. There was a difference between showing up and getting everything done that mattered.

We spent many late nights trying to complete a well. I thought working all day and putting in all the overtime the business required was normal until I got my first apartment at 17. I had a friend who got into a fight with his girlfriend and stayed all night with me. He was in his mid-twenties and was surprised when I left again for work at 10:00 p.m. to check on new wells. I was floored when he told me most people work only eight hours a day five days a week. I was taught business wasn't about a time schedule; business was about doing what needed to be done.

Getting My Start in Electronics

I got married at 21, stopped working for my dad, and moved to California to pursue a career in electronics. I started in the warehouse inspecting and shipping semiconductors. We barely made enough to buy a pizza. I had no credit and couldn't buy a proper refrigerator. We had to buy this two-decade old fridge that almost caught on fire. Maybe we should have repurposed it as an oven.

When I saw the salesroom, I knew that was where the money was made. Within three months I was in. I made calls all day, even late into the evenings trying to broker deals between sellers or buyers, asking what people wanted to sell or buy. After a year I was making $1000 a week. However, the company went through ownership changes and wanted to cut my pay in half. They wanted me to go back to starving. I needed to go out on my own.

I started attending trade shows to broaden my industry knowledge. While at a Comdex show, I met a computer manufacturer that sold Intel math coprocessors at an unusually low price. The math coprocessor was an optional component that could be added to a computer. It enabled the system to solve math problems faster. Today, all computer processors are released with a math coprocessor incorporated into the processor. I knew customers would pay more than his supplier price to add this processor. I saw the opportunity and left my employer in 1985 with my Rolodex, a list of contacts, and cut a deal with the supplier.

I told him I would buy $6,500 a day in parts, drive them around LA selling them, and deposit the checks. However, the catch was I only had $1,700 saved up. I asked him to hold my checks for two business days to make it work. He agreed, and I used that cashflow float to make $500 a day.

The business grew to me shipping fifteen boxes a day out of my apartment working from the kitchen table and sitting on a lawn chair where my butt was falling through. The UPS guy was amazed at all the boxes I was shipping out of my tiny apartment and asked if he could buy stock in my company.

Intel

I wanted to grow the company, but I needed to buy the product directly from Intel. I asked my Intel sales manager incessantly. I would slide my profit and loss statements across the table. He would raise his eyebrows and slide it back. I finally called him on the phone and yelled at him: "I've proven I can sell these by the truckload, and I've been asking you for *six* months. You better make this happen." And I was put in direct contact with Intel the next day.

The minimum order was $10,000 by cashier's check. So the money had to be in the bank before issuing the check. I couldn't float cash as I did before. However, after I bought the first order and paid for it. I noticed afterward that they did not mark the box requiring a cashier's check. So I gave the UPS driver a company check on the next shipment and calculated it took 21 days to clear the bank. I figured if I could sell the parts in that time, I could move as many as I wanted.

Before long I was moving six figures in parts every month. Finally, Intel called me and said I should get a credit line with them. They asked how much I wanted. I thought 10 or 20 grand would be great, but I decided to hold my cards. Here's where the asking comes into play or handy. I said, "How much credit do you think I need?" The credit manager immediately said, "100k." I said that sounded good to me without flinching or jumping up and down (like I was inside). She hit a few keys on the keyboard, and it was a done deal.

Fast forward to now, I own and operate Exit Technologies Inc., an ITAD (IT Asset Disposal Company) company. The way it works is when corporate America gets rid of IT hardware, we protect their brand from data breaches so that the confidential data on the hardware doesn't fall into the wrong hands. The company's brand is worth more to them than the resale value of the used hardware. If credit card numbers or medical information gets out, the damage could be in the millions vs. the hardware's resale value at a few percent of that. Ensuring that information is erased from the data-bearing devices involves tracking the IT assets using ERP software and additional software to wipe the machines. We have highly trained management who continually upgrade the skills of our technicians.

We specialize in data center IT assets. For example, companies such as Facebook, Google and Salesforce have vast amounts of those assets decommissioned every year. Companies hire us to go to the data center and pick up servers and networking equipment racks. We also do refreshes of laptops and desktops. We bring that material to our warehouse, wipe all data, resell the good material, and responsibly recycle the rest.

Not Giving up When Faced with a Death Blow

When my company was small with about 20k in capital, a customer bounced checks on me for most of that amount. I called my dad and told him we were done. My dad and my father-in-law loaned us 10k each. Within six months I paid them off with interest. They had faith in us based on our work history and determination. I remember how surprised my father-in-law was to not only get his money back, but to get interest as well.

Learn From Others

We went on to make 400k the year after we almost closed our doors. There was a computer memory chip shortage that year. Atlas Griffith, who worked for me, knew the Heath Zenith computer stores had stock on the hard-to-find chips. We bought their stock from 21 stores nationwide just before the price skyrocketed. We called a week later, and the store's sales guy said, "You wouldn't believe it, but those chips went way up in price." Apple released the Macintosh without giving it enough memory. So when sales of the Macintosh took off, customers were upgrading the RAM en masse, which depleted the supply, thereby causing the large price increase from $1 each to $11 in less than a year.

Where have you been called to lead? What is the *why* behind what you do?

Now when I go anywhere, even on vacation, I constantly look at the businesses I see. I am thinking of ways to make them better. On one of my trips to Maui, we took a snorkel trip on a three-million-dollar Catamaran. By the end of the day, I had written a two-page report on improving the business and had set up a coffee meeting with the owner to review it. He appreciated it and gave me a few gifts. We became friends, and I'm going out to see him again a year later.

Where Did Your Reinvention or Calling Come From?

When I stopped working in the oil fields, I knew that I wanted to use my brain and mouth, not my hands, to make money. As we drove to California to get my start in electronics, I told my wife that it might change me. I had to become very focused to be successful. Fear is the worst thing, and to this day I still wrestle with it. Working through the pandemic was a good example.

You have to walk in every day like everything is great! Your team will read you and respond. If you are stressed, they will be stressed. We were able to keep working through the pandemic as an essential business, but we thought it would be better to have some people work remotely and reduce the number of people at the office. I then opted to work from home as well. The staff immediately became fearful. So I said, "No problem. I will be there every day."

One of the ways I deal with fear is by getting more knowledge and experience. I have taken Tony Robbins' seminars that built confidence. I got good business advice from Dave Ramsey's EntreLeadership company. They have a saying that the lid to every organization is the leader. If he does not grow, the business does not grow. I am constantly trying new things and working with consultants. Every time I hit a wall, I look for someone to help me get over it. Even recently I realized that I was not good at managing and following through with the things that needed to be done with the business. We have a consultant working and training the three of us for those skills that I was missing and had passed on to some of our staff.

I recently started a podcast and in six months I had interviewed over 20 leaders and visionaries in ITAD. It's called ITADTALK. It started with a phone call from a guy starting a podcast company. He offered me a low rate to be one of his first clients. I thought for a minute and said, "Why not? Let's try it." Even though I was a bit clumsy on air, I took to it and really enjoyed it.

While it did not bring me deals, it allowed me to talk to high caliber people. Some were running billion-dollar companies. It gave me credibility in the industry. It developed my skills of talking to people and drawing them out. I especially like hearing if they were mentored too and are mentoring others. We are obligated to give back when asked for help and advice. That is one of the best feelings I get from helping others grow.

One of the visionaries I interviewed was Chuck Ceccarelli of the Inventive Group. He uses Lean in his manufacturing business. He was a tow truck driver with a $300,000 dollar a year business, who invented a side tow for tow trucks. It allows you to pull a car out of the ditch without blocking both lanes of traffic. He started manufacturing this side pull and went across the country and made over a million dollars in orders.

It took him 13 hours to make the unit, and he wanted to improve that. So he started reading about the Toyota Lean Manufacturing Method and applied what he learned. The end result was a new production time of three hours per unit. He now has a 100-million-dollar business building side tows and does over 50 million a year in sales making many products.

How Have You Been Able to Turn a Setback into a Success?

Last year we had both an increase in payroll costs and a reduction in business. Our clients were not getting rid of as much hardware because they were working from home due to the pandemic, so we had to pivot. I took five of my employees back to Chuck's plant in Idaho, and he and his executive team spent the day showing us how to apply his system. This was in January 2022. We have since realigned our cost structure and are using Lean to make our process more efficient.

You must keep asking yourself whether what you are doing adds value to the customer. If not, it is waste. Lean uses a lot of simple things that may be missed by most companies. One is value stream mapping. You must go to the Gemba (where the work is done) and watch the team members' movements. Where are they walking and what are they reaching for? Time those movements and then ask the team member how we could do this more efficiently. We were able to take many hours out of our processes.

The improvement process never stops; it is a continuous process. When we were at Chuck's, we noticed he had two monitors at every workstation, one showing a diagram or video showing exactly what should be done. The other monitor showed how many minutes it should take to perform that process. One of the things we are implementing now is a software called Trainual. Our operations manager has made a video with instructions for each part of a process. The system keeps track of who completed which trainings. Also, if there is a question, they can look it up. This ensures the process is done the same way every time.

Helping Others

I was at a Joe Dispenza seminar and sat next to a young man at the bar for dinner. He was about 21 and married with a new baby and was struggling about what to pursue as a career to provide for his family. A Facebook group paid for him to attend and change his life. He explained he was an Uber driver putting a thousand miles a week on his car. He had just put a new transmission in his car. He was trying to figure out how to make a better living, one with a future.

I started asking him what he might want to do, what he liked, and what was he good at? He thought about it and did not have an immediate answer. So I suggested doing a service business. I told him that where I lived in Florida everyone must get their houses, driveways, sidewalks, and roofs pressure washed. You can buy a pressure washer for under a thousand bucks, start out on the weekends, and pass out cards in gated neighborhoods, etc.

He said he never thought about starting his own business. He said he didn't have a dad to teach him as I had. I followed up, and he went into real estate. Sometimes asking questions and offering encouragement can help a lot.

It is funny every time I think I know everything, I find out there is still more to learn. I joined a networking group in Naples, where we found our current consultant. One of the business leaders I interviewed on my podcast had used the same type of consultant that was based on the book *Traction* by Gino Wickman. His company is very successful and has over 30 salespeople. It is helping us get rid of trying to do everything and focus on what we are good at. One of the hardest things I must do is to let go of various lines of business. What I'm discovering is when you let go, it frees you up to be better at your core.

What do you want to be remembered for?

- Growth
- Teaching what I have learned to others
- Grit
- Not giving up when faced with a death blow
- Learning from others

How can people connect with you?

I can be found at ExitTechnoloiges.com and on LinkedIn @jeff-bittner-exit.

WE CAN DO HARD THINGS.
WE ARE TOUGHER
THAN WE KNOW.

by Daniel Blum

CHAPTER 6

ONE-MILLION-FOOT-VIEW
BY DANIEL BLUM

What is conditioned from our parents and what is pure pursuit from an inner calling?

I followed my parents' guidance to go to college right after high school. It was the natural progression for someone like me raised in an environment that deemed a four-year degree a necessary requirement for happiness and success.

My father had been a professional soccer player. He guided me towards the American dream of playing professional sports throughout my childhood, prepping and training me for years to become a professional football kicker. But I always knew deep inside, something different, broader, and more expansive was calling me.

As much as I loved playing football, I had a macro vision of the world and humanity. I wanted to explore uncharted terrain, new ideas, and unique perspectives. Thus my burning desire for something more was constantly nudging me to go live outside of social norms.

I had an incredible thirst for knowledge. I would read everything I could get my hands on about the brain, super intelligence, culture, and human behavior. I was intrigued by books geared towards looking at the future, space travel, and solving world problems. My future self was (and still is) on a quest to leave my mark on the world.

Taking all of this in, I had to pick just one major in college. It seemed crazy to me, so I didn't. I thought about becoming a rocket engineer or an evolutionary biologist prior; however, now here I was driving through the wheat fields in Southern Illinois heading to college on a football scholarship, thinking about where I wanted to focus academically once I got there. I decided to go with two majors: agriculture and economics. I figured it would give me a broader perspective and help me gain insights on the ways I could impact the world I was hoping to define. It was a good thing I was thinking broader than just a professional football career. I ended up with mono and my football went on sabbatical.

Four years later, I got my degree. Now, what's next? My father was a driven athlete. He rode his bicycle across the country from Philadelphia to San Francisco in his 20s while in the same decade playing professional soccer followed by a successful sales career.

My mother was always at the very top of her field winning multiple awards in the pharmaceutical industry with a strong drive to succeed, while putting 500 percent effort into everything she did.

Question: Where does our drive come from? Is it genetic?

As I settled into adulthood post college I thought about my place in society and what business ideas I wanted to pursue. I certainly was aware of the drive I had within me to push my body to extremes and desire to excel in business. Was I conditioned by my parents? Most likely. Did I learn to become that because of my environment? Probably. Was I influenced by the books I read? Most definitely.

The books I began reading post college were more geared towards entrepreneurship, vision, and impact. One key theme kept showing up (at least in the books I was reading), that a true entrepreneur's focus should be on building things, fixing things, and making things more efficient, and not have making money as the primary goal. I got it. That hit home for me. Those teachings summed up how I had been feeling all along.

Now here I was in my twenties looking into my unwritten future and trying to figure out who I was and what I wanted to do with my life. I knew I wasn't cut out for a nine-to-five job, so the very first decision I made was to officially become an entrepreneur.

I did a lot of thinking and brainstorming. I had a plethora of ideas. The key question I asked myself was, "What will the world look like in the future and what is my role in building it?" I let my imagination run wild. I began visualizing what technology and artificial intelligence would look like. I prodded, probed, and explored many different options.

During this exploratory stage, I traveled. I lived in Central America. I met new people, and I learned that I was fascinated with different cultures. I am fortunate to have parents who tolerated my need for exploration in my own time and rhythm.

I also started two businesses. The first one was a car transporting company. Just when we were starting to do well, I was blindsided by my friend and business partner who was stealing money on the side. The other biz fizzled out. Neither of the two ended up being long-term.

In 2016, life became intriguing. My friend Brandon, whom I had known for many years, contacted me from Kuwait where he was living and playing basketball. Our interests were strikingly similar—both athletes who did not find fame in sports and had a thirst for knowledge outside our own culture.

The phone call went like this. "Daniel, I want to travel on a school bus overseas for a year, using the bus as my home. No frills, just roughing it. What do you think?" I said, "That's an insane idea. I would love to do that." I said, "Instead of roughing it, why don't we come up with a concept for monetization where we travel on the bus, turn it into a business, learn from the people we meet and then figure out the details along the way?" We were both in.

To get started I came up with a series of ideas, starting with turning the bus into a mobile podcast studio and making it our entire brand. We decided to go to South America to live on the bus for one year driving from the very top to the bottom of the continent interviewing people from all walks of life.

It took us close to a year to put all of the initial pieces of the puzzle together. It was a massive undertaking. First, I had to map out the infrastructure for building out a podcast that would include locating interesting people, learning about the culture, and diving into entrepreneurial conversations.

Phase One: We needed funds to buy the bus and customize it into a living co-working space. We designed a Kickstarter campaign, which successfully raised $17,000. Additional funds came in from selling long sleeve shirts with colorful graphics we had specially designed, and other memorabilia. We sold packages for people to tour with us for a week or two in different locations. In addition we brought in sponsors for the podcast. Money started trickling in.

We knew once we were on the road we could live frugally. All we needed initially was enough to buy and customize the school bus so we could live and work on it.

Phase Two: A month in I realized what we were doing was crazy, which then led to another idea. Rather than just a podcast, we could produce and film an entire documentary series. Of course, we had no idea how to build a film company; however, we did know enough to go on Reddit and find the people who did.

It worked. We connected with two guys who knew film and were willing to hop on the bus and join us traveling through South America. They were in. That's all we needed to start. We decided to go all in and basically build out anything else we needed in the process.

We bought a bus located in Salt Lake City, had it customized, and planned to have it shipped to Columbia, South America via Houston. After a six-week delay due to Hurricane Harvey, the now customized bus was on its way. Brandon and I and the other two guys flew down to move On the Bus, our new business name.

For me personally, it was the first chance I had to get a taste of what it felt like to do something on a bigger scope with meaning. My goals were to do our podcast, meet people, and build a business and a brand. Preplanning was required to attain quality interviews and great YouTube. My propensity for business planning would seemingly be a strong contribution.

For the first seven months of the trip, we were nomads, working 20 hours a day to produce our podcast and video content. When we weren't on our computers or recording digital programming, we were seeking places to live and sleep. Our free time was spent exploring the regions. We met incredible people and had adventures through incredibly beautiful scenery. We were definitely on to something big.

But not all that glitters is gold. Life throws curve balls. It was dicey having four adult men on a bus 24/7. Throw in the business, too. Relationships became rocky. Tight quarters made it difficult. Rough terrain made it even harder. We endured 10 months and then ultimately the trip ended when my partner and I split.

Life is a melting pot of aha moments, epiphanies, and insights. I took a crash course on life lessons traveling through South America without having to read about them in a book. I experienced them first hand. I was completely out of my comfort zone. I almost died several times. I had to solve problems, think on my feet, and face my own mortality. Trust. Hustle. Work hard. Let go. I earned a PhD, metaphorically speaking, in human relationships, business acumen, and patience. Side note, I have a lifetime of crazy stories to share from my experience on the bus.

Where have you been called to lead? What is the *why* behind what you do?

Flash forward to today. I am the co-founder of Alpha-Verse Capital and run a NFT hedge fund. I love what I do, who I get to work with, and how my business fits into my unconventional life.

For those unfamiliar with NFTs, they are digital assets that represent real world objects like art, music, gaming, and videos. They are bought and sold online and have been around since 2014. NFTs are a popular way to buy and sell digital artwork. What many people do not know is that each NFT has a unique coding and are generally one of a kind or part of a very limited run and that makes them valuable.

My intrigue with culture, entrepreneurship, and the artworld led me on the path to the business side of NFTs. Now I get to help creative entrepreneurs grow their impact, influence, and income through Web 3, the metaverse, and NFTs.

How were you able to transform a setback into a setup for success?

The entire On the Bus experience was like Indiana Jones meets Jaws. There was always danger lurking around the corner.

We were growing a following on our podcast and things were running along smoothly in the beginning. In Ecuador, nature wreaked havoc on us. Our bus got stuck inside of a monsoon, next to a volcano, and then under a low overhang during a rainstorm in the middle of Carnivale. We battled the elements and were forced to take the bus through treacherous life or death conditions while pushing ourselves to mental and physical extremes.

Relationships began to unravel. After we crossed the border into Peru, the tensions worsened, and I decided to travel for a bit on my own to the Amazon and the famous jungle city of Acitos to do some podcast interviews. The other guys were just into hiking and adventuring. I was more focused on learning about the culture and producing content. It was a vicarious and complicated trip to get there, and halfway through it I suffered severe food poisoning and could not stop throwing up. Dehydrated and weak, I had no choice but to head back. Meanwhile on the trip back, I fell asleep due to exhaustion and was robbed of my wallet and ID.

It is incredible to say this turned into a success, but my mind was tested in raw survival from the moment we navigated the monsoon, to the fracturing of the temperaments of my traveling companions, to enduring a 48-hour travel with food poisoning to returning to the bus.

Once back and reunited, without the podcast material I succumbed to what the other three guys were up to, which was going on a strenuous hike starting the climb at 11,000 ft heading up to 15,000 ft. Although I probably should have stayed on the bus, I decided to partake. I always pushed my physical limits. I remember part of it vividly when I came up to an area with an incredibly beautiful, unexplainably thin, turquoise-blue river raging to my right-hand side.

It was majestic.

However, right in front of me I saw a pack of adolescent male bulls battling each other. They looked up and took notice of me, and then they stopped and stared. My health was still compromised, and I was too weak to figure out the situation, so I went and sat next to a tree.

After ten minutes next to the tree, the bulls noticed me. They started approaching me and not in a friendly way. Thinking I would walk in the other direction, I stood up and turned around, only to find a gigantic, angry-looking bull staring directly into my face. I tried to go to the left, and another bull approached from the front. They weren't standing back; they were coming at me. My only remaining move was to head over towards the giant rocks. Then a third bull came. The three of them surrounded me, snorting and stomping. Together they had me trapped on all three sides, with my back towards the rocks that had crumbled from the mountain.

There I was in the middle of a foreign continent surrounded by angry bulls. I was exhausted, my head was pounding, and in my mind, this was the end of my journey. I saw no possible scenario in which I would get out of the situation alive. I reasoned that my only option was to get on top of the rocks and prepare to die. I took off my backpack and went to sit down on the rocks in surrender. I then turned to see Brandon, Max, and Tony on the other side of the hill. We made eye contact. It was a centering moment, but it didn't take away from the feeling that I was about to die. The only difference their presence made was that now I thought I would die in front of an audience, and they might catch it on camera.

To try to get the bulls to move away from me they started throwing rocks at them. At first the bulls didn't budge, but after being hit by enough rocks, one of them moved out of my way. I jumped off the rocks and took off running. Once safely back in the bus, I drank a massive amount of THC/CBD concentrate and passed out. A few weeks later I landed in the hospital, where I stayed for the next 10 days. Several weeks later I was back home in the United States.

I learned three important life lessons from this experience:

1. We can do hard things. We are tougher than we know. I made it through this. I can survive other hard things, too.
2. Expect the unexpected. Don't be caught off guard because it will happen. Expect the best but be prepared for the worst in case something really hard hits you. Remind yourself that you can get through it, and you will get through it.
3. Sometimes you have to surrender and let go. My goal was to make it to the Amazon for our podcast interviews. However, I was in incredible pain. I had to turn around and go back. Sometimes you have to know when to surrender and let go. It wasn't in the cards. I almost made it. I am proud of myself for giving it my best effort.

What do you want to be remembered for? What is your ultimate legacy?

My ultimate legacy is to live my life playing full out. I want to contribute to society, learn as much as I can while I am here, be a good human being and say at the very end, "I went all in and made an impact."

How can people connect with you?

I can be found at danielisaacblum.com and on LinkedIn @thedanielblum.

I USE MY SKILLS TO TEACH
PEOPLE HOW TO BECOME
MORE SENSITIVE TO THEIR
REPRESSED FEELINGS,
WHICH ALLOWS THEM
TO RELEASE THEM AND
BECOME FREE TO BE MORE
NATURALLY AUTHENTIC.

by Steven Goldhar

CHAPTER 7

THE SENSITIVE ENTREPRENEUR
BY STEVEN GOLDHAR

Life As a Sensitive Person

As a young teenager, I had a very peculiar experience that began my gradual induction into the realities of a dysfunctional world. It began with my mother asking me to drop off a large, certified check to a lawyer in downtown Toronto. She was looking after my younger siblings and needed to get the deposit for our new house delivered on time. I was 12 years old and felt very proud that my mother trusted me with delivering such an important document. I was excited to visit the financial core of the city, where people go to work and make things happen. It felt like I was on an important mission. I hopped on the subway with the check tucked deep within my sock. The station led me right into the underground walkways of the financial district lined with retail services that snaked through the corridors. It was noon and hungry office workers began streaming through the doors and into the now bustling food courts. I was excited and curious by the activity and the well-dressed people. I began to wonder what each person did when they were up in their office.

Then something inside me began to shift as I observed people more carefully. I was picking up on some strange and uncomfortable energy. It felt cold, serious, and uncaring. The expressions on people's faces weren't happy. I didn't see anyone who looked like they were enjoying themselves or were in a good mood. Isn't lunchtime supposed to be fun, I thought? Isn't this the time we leave work behind and get outside to play and refresh ourselves? Something seemed very wrong, but I had no reference to back up the feelings I was experiencing. I became aware of the tenseness of the energy around me. Some people looked numb or lifeless, and I couldn't read them. No feeling or emotional expression at all. I remember asking myself, "Is this the world I'm expected to grow up and be a part of?" I vowed, in disillusionment that I would never let this happen to me. However, an important seed of adulthood was planted that would shape my experiences and who I became for years to come.

Did you ever look at the world and think that it didn't make sense? I tried my best to keep denying and repressing those feelings, and eventually it led to a very uncomfortable and confusing life experience until I realized when I was older and mature that *I wasn't the problem.* Many years later, I would understand that the cultural system I grew up in has a perfect way of keeping itself reliably running. It teaches us not to feel or fully own and express our feelings, and therefore, we cannot even identify most of our true needs. Sensitive people represent 20 percent of the population and are often the canaries in the coal mine who can sense problems early on. I learned that this was not a welcome trait in a world that often resists change, prefers to defer problems to someone else, and embraces the status quo even if it means pretending to operate in ignorance. My experience in the underground soon faded into the background as I embraced my more comfortable and rational home life, where I played with my friends, watched TV, and went to school.

My Early Entrepreneurial Days

As I matured, I turned out to be quite a young entrepreneur. Self-taught on one of the first computers ever built in the 1980s, by 15 I was working for myself making four times the minimum wage for adults.

At 17, while reading *Entrepreneur* magazine, I became enthralled with the idea of importing and exporting. I formed a company, talked my way through negotiations with a manufacturer in Wichita, KS, and became the exclusive Canadian distributor for his innovative line of air purification products. He never knew how old I was, and I ensured that my mother answered the phone at certain times with my company name, handing me the phone as my acting assistant (Thank you, Mom!).

I took over the garage and brought in my cousin to help. I couldn't have been happier and more excited. I was living with passion and wasn't afraid of anything. I met clients at their workplace and was sometimes invited out to discuss business during happy hour. I had to have a coke as I wasn't old enough to drink. People seemed to respect and take me seriously, despite my age. A year later I became part of a contingency of Canadian companies looking to export to South America. I brought on an older and more experienced partner and together we traveled to attend and exhibit our wares at Expocomer '87 in Panama. I will never forget the look on the face of the Canadian ambassador who had worked with me to organize our booth and trip by phone. When he finally met me in person and saw how young I was (I think I looked about 14 then), his dramatic reaction made me blush.

Life looked exciting and promising, but my life path was destined to be part of a new calling of humans. We're a courageous bunch of pioneering, heart-aligned entrepreneurs whose purpose is to help wake up the planet and move us into the next phase of our collective evolution. Of course, I wasn't aware of this back then. Life events began to show me a different path, wearing me down slowly over the next 20 years, like a piece of steel being forged into something entirely new.

Later that year, I won a high school entrepreneurship award honoring my accomplishments. The award sponsor, a well-known real estate guru, took me under his wing and taught me how to package and sell limited partnership real estate to people of high net worth. Working with this man was very stressful. He trained me army style, degrading me into submission and acceptance of his picture of the world and the way business gets done. My mother could see the damage it was doing to my self-esteem and begged me to quit. I was determined to be strong and finish what I started. I learned how to repress my feelings to become who I thought I needed to be. When we were nearing the closing date of the deal, the man I worked for was away on holidays with his family and a couple of investors wanted to pull out and a couple more had their financing rejected by the bank for not meeting the equity ratio requirements. I ran around town meeting with the investors and the bank and fixed everything and actually saved the deal in the end. It was one of the most stressful times I can remember in my life. When it came time for my commission, he played hardball. I was disheartened and settled in disgust.

My mother saw how stressed I was and convinced me to leave and attend university. The experience of the real estate deal had me doubting myself and whether I was cut out for business. I sold the remaining part of my import/export business and attended undergraduate studies at the University of Toronto.

The Onset of Depression

My twenties were a very difficult period for me. I became depressed in my second year of university and got medical permission to leave. The next year I tried a business program at a different school, and even with straight As in the first term, the same thing happened in the second term, and I left for a second time. Something inside me began feeling more and more like I didn't fit in the world, but I couldn't understand why. I was so bright and competent on one hand and felt alone and disconnected on the other. Where did that talented and fearless young man go? The sensitive part of me longed for more connection and collaboration, but I didn't see any room or possibility to bring these qualities into the professional and competitive path in front of me. I didn't have the support or courage to allow my authentic self to exist at that time and to let my life unfold in the organic way it was meant to. I dealt with that inner conflict by splitting myself off into two parts. One part of me focused on the entrepreneurial and business interests which came naturally to me, while the other part felt sad and delved deeply into personal growth and transformational experiences. I was 25 and felt like a failure, and I continued to live out my life doing the best that I could.

Business, Fatherhood, and ADHD

When I was 29, I moved in with my partner and our son was born. I had just finished my bachelor of science degree and chose to let go of the idea of being a doctor to become a stay-at-home dad to our son and my partner's two daughters, while she worked full-time. I started my next company, Sundance Media, building websites in 1998 and by 2000 shifted focus to become a leading pioneer of online digital marketing. As my business grew, I was cognizant of my continual emotional struggles and limited mental energy and stamina. When I was 34, I was formally diagnosed with ADHD, which helped explain at least some of my struggles. The medications I took dramatically improved the emotional and mental energy issues I had been experiencing. I was good at what I did and landed enterprise clients like IBM, who needed my help to understand the digital landscape. My reputation grew, and I was soon flying to New York to work with one of the world's largest agencies, Ogilvy & Mather, and some of their biggest brands like Ford, Motorola, Walmart, and Kodak.

While my business continued to grow, my relationship with my partner deteriorated. Couples therapy became futile. Neither of our needs were being met. I accidentally found out about her affair and asked for a trial separation after an unsuccessful reconciliation. This triggered a deep abandonment response, which led her to declare war on me. It was like Germany invading the rest of the world. I didn't see it coming, and I wasn't prepared for what happened. This experience could become a movie in and of itself with police, jail, hidden agendas, ongoing drama, deception, and a precious and helpless child in the middle. All the while I was growing my company, had a business partner and employees, and had to keep things running.

I didn't realize that I was suffering from exhaustion. I didn't understand how to look after myself physically, emotionally, or spiritually. I was drawing on borrowed time. More symptoms would arise every year—brain fog, fatigue, stomach problems, and hair and hearing loss. I found a medication for everything—my depression, anxiety, brain fog, stomach, etc. My ADD meds were wonderful at letting me get by with minimal sleep. I worked into the wee hours of the night and was praised by my colleague for my "amazing work ethic." But the symptoms kept progressing until I could barely think straight.

I went to many doctors before they discovered yet another problem. It was confirmed that I was extremely toxic with heavy metals, especially Mercury. They told me that I needed to get regular Chelation IV treatments and that this would be a slow process. My body just gave in, and I couldn't think enough to even work. I had partners investing in my company at the time to expand my business. All of that came to an abrupt end. Within a few months, I couldn't service my debt, so I sold everything I could and moved in with my parents. A year later, I filed for personal bankruptcy, and I felt deep shame.

At that point, my self-esteem was mainly tied to my work success, contacts, connections, and money. I suddenly lost everything in a short period of time. First, my relationship, then my health, soon followed by money and my business. I was bankrupt in every way imaginable. I remember one night I was so scared and in so much pain that I decided to talk to God for the first time in my life. I promised God that I would give up my desires and expectations and just become whatever he wanted me to be. I would live as small of a life as he wanted me to if I could just be rid of this pain. This was my rock bottom.

The Eckhart Tolle Years

Three weeks later, while visiting a long-time friend and teacher of holotropic breathwork I ran into her son, who knew of my online marketing skills and reputation. He asked me for help growing his new business, producing world-renowned teacher Eckhart Tolle and the subscription-based video streaming platform for his teachings. I flew to Vancouver, met with Eckhart and his team and quickly became the director of marketing for Eckhart Tolle TV. Things began turning around quickly. I thrived in the personal growth and transformational space. I could turn my passion into a profession for the first time in my life. I was flying around the world helping put on events and retreats, interacting with deeply passionate and purposeful people and spending countless hours absorbing Eckhart's teachings both from the front row and our friendship. I was promoted to work for Eckhart and his wife directly to help manage some of their other business interests. I began working as a business advisor and marketing specialist for other well-known industry teachers like Gary Zukav, Geneen Roth, and Debbie Ford. I also began working with a colleague on a new project to create a unique online community platform. His experiences with live event programming combined with my knowledge of community building with Eckhart Tolle TV gave us a unique insight into how to build a viable service that would integrate online teachings with ongoing small group and one-to-one interaction. In a sense we were turning learning into an ever-evolving social activity that would be fun and rewarding.

The Cooler Platform

While continuing to build our platform, which we nicknamed the Cooler Platform, I also began to work with New York fashion designer Eileen Fisher. I helped to create a new arm of her business that would teach women (and lucky men like me) to become conscious and empowered leaders. We programmed our events with top-tier teachers like Tara Brach, Gloria Steinem, and Jon Kabat-Zinn.

I participated in every event, absorbing as much transformational wisdom as I could.

Despite the years of exposure working with some of the greatest teachers and healing wisdom available, I still suffered with depression, anxiety, and low self-esteem. I understood self-love conceptually but applying it became elusive. It took a few more years to sensitize to my inner experiences and become self-compassionate. I learned to rebuild my relationship with my many dissociated parts functioning as rogue entities. I discovered that it's in this reintegration work that I could finally become whole again.

The process was both challenging and beautiful and required a commitment to being vulnerable, brave, and honest. I learned to hold my difficult feelings with love and compassion, understand my underlying needs, and let the years of repressed energies finally dissipate. This part of my journey began with a brilliant 12-step program called ACA (Adult Children of Alcoholics and Dysfunctional Families). When Covid hit, the Cooler Platform project ran into financial issues and sadly disbanded. I decided to venture out into a more purposeful and meaningful direction. I have always longed to be in service to others. I did my best to even make it a part of my entrepreneurial experiences by working more closely with clients and even teaching online marketing at schools. I always loved teaching and coaching, but it was merely an adjunct to what I did. I was now inspired to make it part of my core work.

Healthy Love Program

I reconnected with a long-time friend Rachel Levy, a talented and experienced therapist who I knew well from my Eckhart Tolle TV days. Ten years earlier, I had supported her with her business vision of creating the Healthy Love Program, a unique and powerful program designed to bring about personal growth and relationship transformation. Now as a trained coach and with years of business strategy and technical experience we formed a partnership to bring her Healthy Love Program to the next level. The first components of the program were creating The Self-Love Course, The SOS (Secrets of Our Shadows) Workshop and an ongoing weekly program called Healthy Love Sessions. We also both have a strong shared interest in creating community. Together, with knowledge and experience gained from the Cooler Platform project plus Rachel's long-time vision of creating a collaborative community experience, The Nurture Network was born. The first iteration of the platform gave users the ability to meet 24/7 in online rooms on various topics. Live events can also be streamed into the rooms to become an interactive teaching platform. The purpose is to keep users connected with other members.

How were you able to transform a setback into a setup for success?

I finally see the parts of my life—the ups and downs, triumphs and failures, joyful experiences, and painful lessons that have all been ordained to help me see my true purpose and realize my fullest potential. I have made it possible to offer the gifts I've brought into this world—to be a space holder for love, to assist people to see their own potential, to hold themselves in a gentler, kinder way and to accept their feelings, sensitivities and unique traits and challenges, whatever they are. As I went through the difficult process of doing this for myself, I gained a wealth of knowledge and life experiences that help me better understand other people's issues and how to help them. Most of us have learned to repress one of the most important and useful aspects of ourselves, our feelings. This is what guides us through life and leads us to understand our needs. It is part of our source of intuition and creativity and allows us to connect and have empathy and compassion for others. And yet it is the very thing that we are taught to avoid, repress, and ignore at all costs. As a sensitive person I didn't have the luxury of doing this indefinitely, and my journey back to accepting my feelings and all aspects of myself has led me to discover just how valid and important they are to living a more joyful and peaceful life. This is my gift and superpower, my sensitivity to my inner world, which allows me to sense deeply what's going on with people around me. I use my skills to teach people how to become more sensitive to their repressed feelings, which allows them to release them and become free to be more naturally authentic. I have turned the trait that I once hated and hid the most, my sensitivity, into a superpower that sees into the souls of others and guides them back into a life in alignment with their truth and superpower, whatever that may be. Watching people make incredible changes and transformations is the most satisfying and meaningful work I have ever done. Sometimes when I look back, my adult life had a dark cloud hanging over me until I learned to fully accept and embrace all of the unique traits I brought into this life. The Healthy Love Program and The Nurture Network were designed to bring people through the same awakening process in a fraction of the time it took Rachel and me to achieve.

What do you want to be remembered for?
What is your ultimate legacy?

I want to be remembered for the thousands of people I have inspired and helped awaken and for the many connections and relationships I have sparked. I also want to be remembered as a sensitive man who overcame the debilitating and harmful stereotypes passed down and modeled to me. I want to be remembered as someone bold and brave enough to stand out and be different, one willing to embrace collaboration instead of competition and love instead of fear or hate. I want to be remembered for showing people the importance and benefits of embracing our feelings, sensitivities, and inner experiences, and for teaching people how to be in more harmonious relationships, for retaining their uniqueness around others, being able to ascertain and ask for their deepest and most vulnerable needs, regain their ability for compassion and empathy, embrace change in a way that supports their own nervous system, and bring our species out of the longest and darkest days of separation, slavery, inequality, and selfishness. My legacy will be the technologies I bring to fulfill these goals and the individuals I touched who carry the torch of truth and consciousness after me.

How can people connect with you?

I can be found at stevengoldhar.com and on Instagram @sgoldhar1.

YOU CAN'T TAKE IT WITH YOU SO BE PROUD OF WHAT YOU LEAVE BEHIND.

by Maxine Gomez

CHAPTER 8

QUE UNIVERSE
BY MAXINE GOMEZ

Iknew nothing about construction or restoring it, but I woke up one day and decided to start a restoration company. I didn't get the memo that this couldn't be done. I didn't think about a glass ceiling. I put on steel-toe boots and decided this was what I was going to do today.

Since I was a little girl, I have wanted to diagnose and treat disease. In college I was pre-med with a major in neuroscience. My thesis was on the biochemical effects of food on mood via neural transmission, literally that we are or we feel what we eat. With a minor in medical anthropology, I believe I could show that if we understood our individual body makeup, genes, Vedic body type, blood type, and personality, we could understand how a person could get what they needed to excel, perform, and function at their optimum, body, mind, and soul.

Before college, I studied with medical practitioners from East to West. I studied with Native American shamans in sweat lodges, witches with healing potions, acupuncturists, even completed Reiki III and became a master practitioner, read everything by Carlos Castaneda, and interned for Dr. Garcia, the orthopedic surgeon who brought the spinal cord disc replacement surgery through FDA approval. Every part of this was equally important; it was all a way to understand parts of every individual.

My mother is a healer and truly has the magic touch. I can say, without bias, that people have traveled from all over the world to be healed by her. She applies the same magic to being a mother. My father is an engineer, measure twice, cut once. He uses the same practicality in being a father. I have been blessed to fall right down the middle. So naturally I wanted to fix people. Sigh. I learned, however, that you can't fix people; people have to want to be fixed, and they have to do most of the work themselves. But I could fix buildings, and people lived in buildings, so I could still help people.

Step one in starting a business is to find someone already doing it well, and then find a way to improve the process. Somewhere in between *not* starting the medical DO program and starting the restoration company I was the co-founder of a retail product launch: Swipes Lovin Wipes Inc., an all-natural, eco-friendly, adult wipe for before and after intimate moments. It was biodegradable, compostable, flushable, and pH balanced for the pink parts. Say that five times quickly. I did at every elevator pitch, trade show, and buyers meeting. We sold to Walgreens, Whole Foods, and adult store distributors. Before starting, I knew nothing about retail. We did our research, learned everything I never knew I needed to know about manufacturing paper products—where and how they are made—how each big box retail store has its own language, and that they won't speak to you without a translator. It was an expensive lesson. It is true what they say that every overnight success takes five to ten years. Three years into the launch, it had legs. Then two things happened: it became an order taking business, and I broke up with my boyfriend with whom I had started the company. We had a partner, another couple, and because of his spite they fired me.

The night I left my home of ten years, I went to the beach. I know, I know, cliche, but yes, the ocean has always been a place of resolve for me. It was late, and I wandered along the beach until I ran into a woman I recognized from yoga. She was sitting alone, and I asked if she was OK. She smiled, then looked at my swollen, teary face and asked me to sit down and if *I* was OK. She shared with me how she had left a difficult marriage and found peace in herself, which was the hardest but also the best thing she had done. Mid-sentence she stopped her story and said, "You see those red lights? Run over there quietly and as fast as you can." I did. Turtles were hatching. They would poke their head out, do a little dance, and then being guided by the moonlight they would find their path to the ocean. I always knew I had a gift, a calling, but this was the first spark. Cheese, I know, but when you can't deny it anymore, you can start to sprinkle your magic.

Broken-hearted and penniless, I went to my parent's house. As a team, I built the business, and he managed the finances at home. I left with nothing but my clothes in bags. While I am forever grateful for my parents' graciousness and open arms, this was my rock bottom, and I was just lucky I had a soft landing.

I laced up my first pair of steel-toe shoes, put my hair in a bun, and got to work. I was hardened, and this line of work made me tough. We provided water, mold, fire, and crime scene clean up services. You know, all the fun stuff. It wasn't pretty, and it smelled even worse. It is definitely *not* like what you see on TV. It was mostly catastrophic. Clients and team members were always stressed. I was determined to bring a woman's touch to the business and was almost always able to answer with a smile and stay calm while every caller thought it was the end of the world. It paid the bills. I found companies doing the work and looked for areas to improve. I did it again, rinse and repeat. I hired people who knew more than me and brought them to work on my team. They were happy to get paid and not think about handling the business side. And I was happy to learn from them and put their skills to work. This is where I shine, connecting the dots.

My first team members came by referral, or I poached them from other job sites. I had hired a drywall team to run a job for me, most of them spoke Spanish but did not know I did. The first day I went to do my surprise walkthrough I heard a few of them talking about me in Spanish. You know the kind of talk I am talking about, locker room talk. One guy cut them off and said, "Esa no, esa es la Jefa." Not that one. She is the chief. They looked down at their boots and went back to work. I approached him after the day was done and offered him a job. I knew if he would protect me without knowing me, then he would be loyal once he did. I promised him that he would eat before I did, and as long as he gave me 40 hours a week, I would take care of him. He did, and I kept my promise. Little by little, we grew, and he brought more of his people to work with me, earning me the title, Senorita Jefa, little miss chief.

I had gone from pre-med to serial entrepreneur and learned through bootstrapping. A friend of mine told me about a program for entrepreneurs. I kept telling him I was too busy. For two years he insisted until one day, he said, "If you are too busy, then you are doing it wrong." That hit me. I was exhausted. I didn't fully understand the metrics of my business, and while I was good at keeping the lights on, I wasn't getting ahead. At the time I had no idea how I would afford the membership. But I was desperate and leaped.

The first meeting they asked us to put away our phones. Instantly the panic set in. I told them that was impossible for me because I run an emergency services company and calls come in all the time, and I couldn't miss a call. At the time I was saying yes to every job. They explained that this was the goal, to step away from working in the business to working on it. I didn't believe them because I had the limiting belief that I had to work hard. But, as always, I have tried to surround myself with those who know more than me, and here they definitely had their act together. Everyone in the room had to qualify by revenue. They were calm; I was only calm on the outside.

From that first meeting it was obvious to me that my friend was right; I was doing it wrong. I was wearing every hat, literally: the hard hat, the owner hat, the technician, the assistant, sales, marketing, billing, *every* hat. How could I be so wrong? I would come home tired and dirty every day. That meant I was working hard. So that had to mean I was doing it right. I was so wrong.

Again, I had no idea how, but I trusted. I drank the Kool-Aid and followed the program. I learned how to scale. I could not wear every hat and expect to succeed. I had to put people in their strengths and build a team. To qualify for many of these construction jobs I needed to legitimize the business, have proper documentation, insurance, workers' compensation, you know, all the fun stuff. One thing I am good at is connecting the dots whether it be people or paper work. I studied for my FL state mold license and took it one step further and was later certified to teach mold remediation. It gave me the knowledge and the credibility in a competitive market, and I enjoyed learning something every time I taught. I love teaching, connecting the dots in their mind, getting the job done right, and working smart, not hard. I registered for all the accolades: small, emerging, Hispanic, minority, women-owned businesses. Registered with every municipality and vendor profile. The trick is to get your name on the list, then it's not if they will call, but when. Now I was on every list.

As we grew, I came to the difficult realization that I could not legitimize all of my team. I told them I didn't care how they did it, but they would have to bring me papers for us to continue working together. I lost a few good men. Very good men.

By now, I knew enough to train people and started hiring again. One of my first legit hires was referred to me by a friend, a psychologist. As it turns out he was a ward of the state. He played football in high school and had a full ride to play ball in college. When he wasn't drafted to play pro, his foster family closed the doors on him, and his support ran out. He was now an adult with nowhere to go. I hired him. At the very least, I knew he was used to listening to a coach, could take instruction, and was hungry. He lived out of his car but showed up to work every day.

I gave him a backpack with some essentials for hygiene. I called it the dignity kit. I lied and told him everybody got one when they started work. It wasn't true then, but it was then after. No questions asked. If you could show up, I would get you started. I'd have healthy snacks and would take him to lunch when I could. He started getting his confidence back, getting on his feet, saving money. Then his family started asking him for things. The pressure was too much. He turned to drugs, and he quickly deteriorated. Despite my best intentions and support, I was not equipped for this. He started selling drugs and taking them and slowly stopped showing up for work. One day he got in his car and went down I-95, going at full speed in the wrong direction until he hit a wall. He died on impact. He had suffered so much throughout his life. I could only pray that now he was at peace. He deserved better.

This was my call, to connect the dots and put people in their strengths so that they may live a fulfilling life. I promised myself I would do better.

I remembered I had taken an assessment when I started teaching with NORMI (national organization of remediators and mold inspectors). This assessment was called, "Strengthsfinder" by Tom Rath. I found mine. The same sign that hangs above the Oracle in the *Matrix* that reads, "Temet Nosce," "Know thyself," hangs in my office.

Positivity, Woo, communicator, adaptability, assurance, and relator, these are my core strengths. Yup. Can't fight it. I am who I am, a dot connector. I put everyone on the team through this assessment. For most of them it was the first time they could reflect on their own strengths. Each person loved what they read. They could identify with what they were good at. Something clicked, and it made sense for them. They were happy that someone took an interest in them and that they could focus on what they innately excelled at. Most companies don't focus on their people or their strengths. They simply hire and hope the body can do the task. I coached them individually and helped them set goals for the job and their life outside of work. By understanding them and their strengths, I had technicians who ended up in sales. I shuffled people around on the organizational chart by their strengths and not by their skills. We had grown men cleaning mold and brains who were happy with their work. Skills I can teach; strengths you are born with.

I received a call from a friend who works with disadvantaged girls in LA. She asked if I would speak to them. I said I think you have the wrong number. I am a blue-collar worker just keeping my head above water. She said, "Yes you are, but you're also a Latin woman

CEO of a construction company. These young ladies need to know someone has laid the path for them."

It had not occurred to me. I had always felt fearless because the road had already been paved before me. I don't have to ask if it is possible. Someone has already paved the path. I knew I just needed the right pair of shoes. I never thought I could be that for someone else.

I could finally unlace the steel-toe boots. I could soften. Finally, I was in a place where I could work on the business, not just in it. And my steel toes turned to boss heels, #steeltoesandstilletos. I recognized the disconnect between so many amazing organizations and businesses needing trained people. Everyone was working so hard in their lane that they couldn't slow down to see the other. Insert dot connector. I've been working with the Adult Education Coalition, The Immigration Reform Committee, Career Source, Boys and Girls Club, and many more that just needed someone outside to see how to bridge their efforts. I didn't just want to connect the dots; I wanted those dots to dance. I like to say I learned to dance and roll with the punches.

While taking lessons on the dance floor, I met Rachel, a patron of love. She helped me see how hard I had been on myself so I could practice healthy love. Learn, unlearn, relearn. But you can't remove your experience no matter how hard you try; believe me, I have tried. What had cultivated from my experiences was tough love. Once I stopped fighting it, I could believe. I know, nothing is impossible, but you have to put action into it. It is not as bad as it sounds. Tough love is just love with action. It means going from feeling to doing. Tough love means to have the resilience to handle discomfort with grace.

To meet your needs, to be afraid but to do it anyways, knowing I'm standing right behind you to give you the push, the cheer, the victory dance.

Today I get to meet people where they are. We hope to prevent a whole segment of the population from falling through the cracks of our system and equip them with the skills to be empowered as they find career paths in rewarding jobs with great companies. We also aim to help companies find the much-needed talent and for this, I can wear any shoes.

I am not the hand holder; I am an ass-kicker. I am the steel toe, tough love department.

Where have you been called to lead? What is the *why* behind what you do?

We were raised in communities that understand it is our duty to give if we are able to. Like many blue zones, people with a sense of purpose live longer. It is not only a calling. It is not altruistic. There is the need not only to survive but also to thrive to ensure that the next generation of our tribe excels. A call to lead is not to attract followers but to create more leaders. To lead is to inspire others to be fulfilled. This is my why, not just to survive but to dance. If I have survived, it is my calling to give back.

How were you able to transform a setback into a setup for success?

For most of my adult life it felt as though for every one step forward I had to take two steps back, cha cha cha. It wasn't until I started working in my passion that things started to fall into place. Working in your passion doesn't have to be dramatic; it can be the simple pleasure of doing what you enjoy and have strength in. When so many things went wrong, I could find the solutions to make it right. This is why today I coach and teach the tough love department and why I work in education to set up others for success.

What role does collaboration have in your current business?

You cannot do it alone, period. Are you the best at what you do? Even the best athletes have coaches. What makes you think you can't benefit from one? The quarterback cannot also be the running back. The main singer cannot also be doing lights and sound. The first thing you need to know are your own strengths and weaknesses. What do you love to do and what are you good at? What do you hate doing and are not good at? Do what you love and delegate what you don't love. There are many things I am not good at. I can focus on what I am good at. Know your numbers. We are the bottlenecks of our business. The more you grow, the more your company will grow. Running your own business requires getting out of your comfort zone and having tough love to push you past your fears.

What life or business lessons have created the most growth for you?

Cut your losses, hire slowly, and fire quickly. Clap for yourself. Nobody Cares. Work harder. Nothing is impossible. You will never lose money by making a profit. Don't aim for a bigger piece of the pie; aim to create a bigger pie. Pie by yourself is lonely. That is why it is meant to be sliced. Be curious. Be kind. Be grateful. Be the dumbest one in the room. Ask questions. You can't take it with you so be proud of what you leave behind. And just in case nobody told you today, good morning, I believe in you. You're doing great.

What do you want to be remembered for? What is your ultimate legacy?

I am grateful for the blessed life I live, and I honor it by living it to the fullest. If my life and experience can inspire others to know that they can pursue their passion, then I would be humbled to be remembered as such.

How can people connect with you?

I can be found at www.drytech27.com and on Instagram @drytech247.

I BELIEVE THAT FAITH
GIVES US HOPE AND THAT
HOPE IS WHAT IGNITES
THE FLAME FOR CHANGE.

by Julia Langley

CHAPTER 9

MASTER LUCRATIVE COMMANDING PERFORMANCES GLOBALLY WITHOUT FEAR BY JULIA LANGLEY

For 17 years I worked for Cirque du Soleil as a featured singer, traveling to over 20 countries and all 50 states in the US. I started performing at the age of two and performance art became part of my fiber, my very being. I consider myself to be fortunate to have found my talents and my tribe at an early age and to go into adulthood with knowledge and experience. There is no better feeling than to be able to do what you love as a career.

Being in a different city every week, expensive costumes and makeup, signing autographs, press photos, and media spots were all part of the job. Standing ovations, show after-parties, and seeing your name in lights makes the job as exciting and as glamorous as it appears from the outside. However, the shadow side of that is both demanding and rigorous, taking its toll physically. There are sacrifices to be made, and when setbacks come, they can bring even the toughest performer to their knees. This is exactly what happened to me the morning of March 21, 2019.

I woke up in a great mood, on top of the world. I was in the best physical shape of my life, performing all over the world, making great money, and enjoying the South Florida tropical lifestyle of boating and beaches when I wasn't traveling. When I left my house on that sunny morning to get my oil changed, I had no idea that my life would be taking a different turn. It was one moment that completely derailed me onto a surprisingly unfamiliar path.

That fateful morning, I dropped my car at the oil change shop and jumped on my bike to go get coffee. I would never get to taste that coffee because as I pedaled in the bike lane, I was broadsided by a monster of a jeep as I crossed an intersection.

I was a careful biker. I stopped and looked both ways. I never ran out in front of traffic. Sometimes things just happen to us.

I don't remember the impact, but I do recall the grill of the jeep bearing down on me two inches from my face and the thought that I might not survive washed over me like a flood. I remember feeling panicky at first, the screams, and then just feeling resigned as I watched the jeep approach. My body twisted through the air like a distorted gymnast (a feeling that comes back to me occasionally when my balance is off or when I am flying in a plane), and I can recall hearing the dull thunk when the back of my head hit the pavement.

The next thing I remember is being put in an ambulance and crying to the EMTs because they had to cut my $20 shirt off of me. I was in shock, but because I was a performer, I kept thinking I needed to hold it together, until I realized that they were talking about how badly my speech was slurred and that they couldn't understand what I was saying. I went blind, my eyes closed, and I started screaming, horrified, but no one could hear me. I was paralyzed, trapped inside my own body. And for the second time that day I thought, "This is what dying feels like."

When I was released from the hospital, I was diagnosed with a spinal cord injury. I had several herniated discs and one in particular was pushing on my spinal column. They aren't sure what caused my temporary paralysis in the ambulance, but they were certain if I didn't have spinal cord surgery, I would be paralyzed. I was released with a follow up to schedule surgery. Unfortunately, 85 percent of my injuries were undiagnosed.

I tried to drive but would become disoriented and couldn't remember where I was. I couldn't say the names of common items on the counter. My doctor stopped me from driving and diagnosed a traumatic brain injury from the impact with the jeep and the ground. It was also discovered since I couldn't walk or use my hands that I had five broken bones. As with most full body trauma, as you get better in one area, another injury starts to show up, and the doctors diagnosed a torn hip labrum and a detached shoulder tendon. It would require surgery to fix both.

The physical injuries were overwhelming, but the mental and emotional toll was even worse. I stopped sleeping, and when I did sleep, I would have nightmares. About three months after the accident, the panic attacks started, and I was particularly triggered by unexpected loud noises. It was then that I discovered that I had PTSD, and I would spend the next few years learning how to manage that, along with the additional surgeries that were required. I lost my motivation and drive. I had no energy or strength to walk much less go to the gym. I felt as though I had no advocates, and my whole life was just a fight to no end. I had so much fear: fear of riding my bike, fear of having a panic attack when I walked out on stage, fear that my knee would collapse when I started to sing, fear of walking across the street. And I feared that I would live in pain forever. But I made the decision that I would learn to adapt, and I was not going to continue to live in that place of weakness. I was a performer, and I was strong. I just needed to find it again.

Reborn – I believe that faith gives us hope and that hope is what ignites the flame for change. Instead of letting my physical limitations win, my anxiety and fear overtake me, and giving up my life of performing, I made a conscious decision to use those gifts to impact the world. I live by the quote, "To whom much is given, much is required." If we are blessed with talents, wealth, knowledge, and time, it is our duty to share those gifts to benefit others.

To say that I recovered would be incorrect. You don't survive a trauma and go back to what you were before. If I measured it by that, I would continue to have a negative perception. I have physical limitations now. After three surgeries and a head injury, I forget things more often. Sometimes my knee gives out and I fall. I can't attend rock concerts (one of the things I loved to do with my friends) because the noise is unbearable and sometimes, I feel panic when I cross the street on my bicycle. But I don't measure my success by those things anymore. I didn't recover; I was reborn. Reborn to use my new strengths and wisdom, and to emerge into the best and most productive period of my life. A period of my life that reaches far beyond myself, and into the lives of others so that they may reach their dreams and impart their own change in the world. But to impart that change, to make that movement happen, you must confront your own fear and summon all of the strength that you have available.

What is your monster? My accident gives new meaning to the tongue-in-cheek phrase, "I feel like I've been hit by a car." And I still jokingly say this. In all seriousness, though, I ask you to take a minute and think about what your monster jeep looks like. Maybe your jeep was a horrific divorce or grief from the loss of a loved one. Maybe your jeep is a paralyzing fear that keeps you from achieving your goals, or maybe it is childhood abuse. Everyone has a treacherous jeep in their life, and for each person it is different, but there is one thing we all have in common, and that is how our challenges and fears affect our confidence.

We start to question ourselves. "Who am I to do this?" "What if I fail?" "What will people think?" We weaken ourselves with statements like "I don't deserve to make lots of money," "I won't win," "I'm too old," and "I'm not good enough."

I have made every single one of those statements at some point in my journey, and I have also been stuck in a place where I felt so overwhelmed that I feared I would never dig my way out. When I'm in that place, I love to think about the words from the song "Tomorrow" from the musical *Annie*, written by Charles Strouse and Martin Charnin.

"When I'm stuck with a day, that's gray, and lonely
I just stick out my chin, and grin, and say
The sun'll come up tomorrow

So you gotta hang on til tomorrow
Come what may
Tomorrow
You're only a day away"

Opportunities Not Obstacles -How were you able to transform a setback into a setup for success?

Several years have passed now, and as I look back on the trials and the strength it took to push through them, I celebrate the anniversary that I lived! March 21, 2019 has become the date that I was given a second chance—a chance to see the world in a new way, a chance to love a little harder, a chance to be more grateful, a chance to impact the lives of others, and a chance to make the future what I want it to be. I honestly can't say I'm glad the accident happened, but I can say that it set into motion a chain of events that has given me prosperity, a new perspective, the freedom to work from anywhere I choose, and my favorite, the opportunity to forge a new era in my career. I could have given up. I had a real reason to stop, but I didn't. I turned a major setback into a setup for success. And I have been rewarded handsomely with amazing new connections, a strong conviction, and a plan for the future.

One of the greatest gifts that I received after my accident was the gift of time. Time to better care for myself in a way that I had not been doing. I was able to spend time with my aging parents. I ate breakfast with my dad and drove him to his domino games. I had the honor of taking care of him before his sudden passing in 2021. My accident also gave me time and motivation to look at my career, plan where I wanted to go, and begin taking action towards a new future. That new future included taking years of knowledge, skill, and experience in performing and using it to help others learn to give commanding performances by overcoming fear. It isn't just the mission of my coaching program, Performing for Success; it is my passion and my commitment to make my second chance at life count.

Fighting the Fear - Fear of public speaking is the number one fear in the world, and it affects 76 percent of the population. I've experienced that fear, and I know how debilitating it can be. Fear holds us back in all areas of our lives but can be particularly toxic when we are faced with an opportunity to perform. To be a successful performer, you must be vulnerable, personal, and authentic, which opens an individual up for a lot of painful criticism. The lines become blurred between the job you have to perform and your personal self. Fear shows up in our posture, in the sound of our voice, our breath, where our eyes are focused, our ability to formulate sentences, our willingness to communicate, to try new things, and to push our potential. When left unchecked, fear starts to creep, like slime on a dirty pond. It starts out small and before you realize it, it has a complete chokehold, stifling creativity, imagination, authenticity, and any new idea that might rise to the surface. The good news is fear can be controlled and used to fuel our energy for success.

Where are you with your fear? What kind of fear is getting in the way of you giving a commanding performance or presentation? To admit you have fear makes you vulnerable. It's a risk to answer the questions that expose the parts of us that we want to hide. But let's be honest here. It is a much bigger risk *not* to ask those tough questions of ourselves. The bigger risk is missing an opportunity to share your story. It's missing the standing ovation when you perform in front of a group. You are risking your goals, your wealth, and your dreams.

Instead of "Who am I to do this?" Ask yourself, "Who am I *not* to do this?" Instead of "What if I fail?" Ask yourself "Seriously, what is the worst that could happen?" Replace "What will people think" with "I'm the courageous one for trying something new."

Resilience is kryptonite for fear. When we start asking ourselves the right questions, we rediscover our tiny seed of strength, and we take a small step to move forward. The resilience muscle begins to grow, and then we find more strength and take bigger risks, and the cycle continues. Eventually that tiny seed will burst forth with strong, colorful, confident blooms, and we can step on stage with knowledge, skill, and the confidence to be successful.

Performing for Success Evolution - How have you pivoted, shifted, or expanded in your business in the last few years? Before my accident I was best known as an international singer and vocal coach. My vocal clients were from all parts of the world with different backgrounds and disciplines, but I started to see similar changes in them as they committed themselves to the program. I started witnessing a personal power emerge as they learned how to use their voice. They discovered things about themselves, what they liked, how they fit into the world, self-worth, and their ability to do hard things.

Quite often when people think of performing, the definition is limited to a person onstage that is participating in arts, such as singing and dancing for the entertainment of others. But I began to realize when I coached clients in the Performing for Success program, they received more attention for their performances and increased their income. Their confidence started to grow, and they stepped out of their comfort zone frequently to dominate the stage and win awards. Performing for Success wasn't just helping singers; it was creating leaders, speakers, business owners, teachers, actors, and real estate professionals by helping each individual discover their unique strengths and using them to give a commanding performance. It was then that I realized Performing for Success wasn't just a vocal coaching program but a life-altering, transformational program that was equipping people to pursue and achieve success.

Seeing how much impact performance training was having on people's lives, I started looking at ways that I could make a bigger impact and reach more people. Performing for Success was no longer just a singing program, but was redesigned and expanded to help speakers, singers, and other high-achieving performers overcome stage fright and give powerful, lucrative performances on a global scale.

Where have you been called to lead? What is the *why* behind what you do?

The driving force behind Performing for Success is the people. As I watch the changes in my clients, I am always filled with wonder and awe. One client suffering from paralyzing, nauseating fear and hiding in the bathroom, transformed into a confident, empowered woman standing on the stage and telling people why they should choose her as the representative for their state. A once awkward, insecure individual discovered musical talent he never dreamed he had inside of him and turned it into a thriving career. Another example is an adult in midlife who found her personal power after being told from childhood to adulthood that she wasn't good enough. These are just a few of the transformational changes that have happened as result of the Performing for Success coaching program.

What do you want to be remembered for? What is your ultimate legacy?

As I think back on certain moments in my life's journey, I realize that there were specific moments that completely changed the trajectory that I was on. My bicycle accident is but one example of a life-changing moment. What I find truly amazing, though, is that most of these moments are not recognized while we are living them. It is in reflection that we find just how important a moment was.

Several years ago I wrote a song entitled, "The Moment" and the whole premise of that song is about stepping out of our comfort zone and having the courage to present our truth when the moment comes. We give in to fear, and it stops us from using our God-given voice, and that pivotal moment in our life completely passes us by, but it doesn't have to!

I believe in a world where people find their voice and use it for good. I believe in a life where fear takes a backseat to confidence. I believe in a purpose that transforms lives and brings dreams to fruition.

I want my legacy to be about helping others stop fear in its tracks and respond powerfully when their moment of opportunity is presented.

As Performing for Success continues to evolve into the premier training program for speakers, singers, and other high achievers, my hope is that principles such as resilience, empowerment, champion, commanding, abundance, fierceness, impactful will be passed on to other change-makers and leaders.

There will never be an ideal time in your life to make a commitment to yourself to take action. There will always be reasons why you shouldn't do it. But the reward is so much greater than the risk. You have a unique talent burning inside of you. You may not realize it, but there is always someone looking to you for guidance, support, and direction. Will you be the person who stands up and says, "I am good. I am strong. I can do hard things and so can you," or will you be the person that hides behind your fear and lets it dictate your success? We have the freedom to choose a life of more freedom or a life of being bound by the chains of fear that we have created in our own mind. Are you ready to make the powerful decision to use your voice, overcome your fear, and perform in the world with confidence and strength? If you are, it's time to lean in and unleash your power.

"Confidence thrives when fear is conquered."

How can people connect with you?

I can be found at JuliaLangley.net and on Instagram @cirquesinger.

LIFE GETS BETTER WHEN YOU SHARE AND ESPECIALLY WHEN YOU SHARE IN COMMUNITY.

by Eileen Lemelman

CHAPTER 10

I DIDN'T DIE AT 60
BY EILEEN LEMELMAN

L ife suddenly and unpredictably changed; in an instant everything was different. We all were in lockdown, at home waiting to be told "OK, all clear. You can come out of your houses now," but the announcement never came.

I am a licensed clinical social worker/ psychotherapist, and I was treating patients day after day who were scared, alone, anxious, and depressed. Technology, oh, thank goodness for technology, allowed me to continue working and helping my patients. I was so happy that therapy provided a safe space for people, and they could emote and cry and yell and shake in fear. I was able to be the voice of peace and calm and reason and hope during a very dark period in our lives. And as I worked with my patients in meditation, breathwork, journaling, talking, and crying, I started feeling something shift in me. I had an epiphany, an awakening!

Fear kept showing up. Fear can show up at any stage of life, no matter what you have or have not accomplished. Actually, what continually surfaced over and over again for my patients was the fear of dying. My patients were afraid to die before seeing family, before crossing off items from bucket lists, before living full meaningful lives, and before connecting to lost dreams. I had an uncomfortable, familiar feeling inside of me. My feelings were getting triggered as well as theirs. At the same time that my patients were wondering if there would be a tomorrow, a future, a life, I became aware that my own beliefs about death and dying started stirring inside of me. The belief system from my childhood was calling to me.

If we had met in February 2020, it would have been in my office for an hour, lunch packed, gas tank full, business dress attire. But somehow losing the structure of driving to an office and having human contact left me unsettled and honestly somewhat adrift. I was losing my way and beginning to question the value of my one-on-one therapy sessions with patients. I knew I was helping my patients, but somehow the isolation of Zoom was not feeling meaningful, and the loneliness made me yearn for more. I was starved for human contact, but I was starved for more. But what would that look like, feel like, be like? What would that really mean for me? Was I too old? Was it too late to begin a new chapter? Was my mother right that life ends at 60? How much change is actually possible for a 60-year-old woman?

Again, that familiar voice was getting louder. I started having a dialogue with myself. What are you thinking? Are you crazy? You are not young enough, smart enough, technologically savvy enough. Oh yes, all the not enough thoughts began lecturing me as to why I should not think of making any changes in my life, especially in midlife. You should be thinking about retiring, not starting a new endeavor. Oh yes, now I know who was saying no to me. Hmmm that sounds like the admonishments of my mother. "Just exist by waiting, waiting to die and not pass 60," mom would say.

In the midst of a pandemic, facing the possibility of dying I found myself searching for more. I was longing for change. I was trying to find meaning out of this scary and chaotic time. There was a collective energy at that time, an anxiety field of energy that was felt in the environment. I realized that I was straddling two worlds. The world in which my mother taught me that life ends at 60 and you should not expect to live beyond those years colliding with the world of limitless possibility at any age, the world that was crying out to me for normalcy, connection, and hope. My soul was calling me to transform and change, and I knew I was not alone because I observed so many women asking the same thing. What is life all about? What is my life's purpose? Is this all that I can expect to have? And a very important question...What do I want? What do I really want? Did you ever ask yourself that question? Can you ask yourself what it is that you want in this life? Does it feel selfish and greedy? So many women don't ever ask themselves either because they were not taught to do so or do not feel they have permission to ask that very important question. *What do I want?*

I had a vision to create a platform, a community, a safe place for women who were struggling and in pain, experiencing highs and lows, joys and fears, uncertainty and loss. A place where women could see other women just like themselves and share their stories. I want to speak to women who think that their life is over and has come to an end.

So I did the only thing I could do. I channeled Oprah! I knew I had to go big, bigger than one-on-one sessions and bigger than group therapy in an office.

The online TV show called *It All Starts with You* was born out of a hope to empower, encourage, inspire, and support women to show up for themselves at any age. In order to truly know who you are, you cannot hide in fear from yourself and from others. The pandemic gave us all the perfect excuse to hide and stay isolated. I must admit that I had fears and limiting beliefs about starting over and creating a new path for my life. I had self-doubt. I questioned whether I could learn the new technology required and vital in business today. I contracted a local production studio and decided to tape my shows for all the world to see. It was terrifying. I felt so vulnerable, but I thought "I am in." I have always been someone who took risks like when I opened my private psychotherapy practice with no patients to fill up my schedule, or when I made the decision and convinced my husband to move to Florida from New York, leaving everything we had ever known, but we knew that we needed a change. My motto in life has always been "Jump in and figure it out later." I jumped in feeling naked and exposed, but I did it anyway. My goodness, a therapist on TV? Yes, it was definitely out of the box. My soul was definitely calling me to help women find their voice (the voice that society tells us to mute and the voice that was considered odd in my own family). And women were watching!

My message of hope and encouragement and inspiration resonated with women. My heart started singing as I creatively and intentionally was helping so many.

I am so grateful for leaping out of my comfort zone. But how did I transition into a leadership role? What are the steps for living a passionate, vibrant, meaningful, and purposeful life? I used a three-pronged approach that I call I.A.G.

Number 1
" I " Intentions

Set intentions every day. How do you want to show up every day? Intentions guide your actions, your thoughts, and your responses as you move through your day. They are different from goals, which are future oriented. Intentions are present, mindful, and in the moment. I encourage you to create a manifesto for intentional daily living. I created a manifesto that kept me focused and present every day. This is my manifesto.

I choose to be.
I choose to be confident in myself and my purpose and my journey.
I choose to be happy and joyful.
I choose to be calm and peaceful.
I choose to be able and competent.
I choose to be a model of honesty and integrity.
I choose to be so successful.
I choose to be full of life.

Number 2
"A" Action

You must move.
Take a step even if that step is scary. Have you ever asked yourself, "Why do I feel so stuck in my life?" All change starts with

one step. Tony Robbins tells us that "motion creates emotion." Movement changes your mental state and breaks negative patterns. One step is progress and progress is the key to happiness. Many say that I am their personal cheerleader on my show and highlight their accomplishments as they break through from being stuck." You need to be your own cheerleader. So get moving and cheer yourself on with A-C-T-I-O-N! Finally, and maybe the most important...

Number 3
"G" Gratitude

Let appreciation and gratitude fill our hearts with the knowledge and wisdom that it is such a privilege to be here and be a human being on this earth. Close your eyes and breathe. Feel your personal energy. Inhale and exhale. Do not take it for granted that you are here and still breathing. With all that you've have been through, you are here, and you are breathing on this incredible day.

That is the foundation. That is the meaning and purpose in life. To bring your purpose back to your breath, have the courage to take a risk on yourself by taking one step in a community that supports you.

What is your passion? What stirs your soul and makes you feel in total harmony with why you showed up here in the first place. The only thing that will keep you from playing the music you hear and marching to the unique drumbeat you experience is fear. According to the Course in Miracles, there are only two basic emotions. One is fear and the other one is love. You may fear the risk of stepping out of the comfort zone of what others determine is your mission and purpose in life. You may fear the unknown but take that step anyway. Women have often lived a life that is limited and small. So success and happiness might be scary. The only way to challenge these untrue notions is to go towards what you know you are here for and let success, joy, and happiness chase after you as it most assuredly will when you live your purpose.

I want to dispel the myths of failure and turn the moans of despair and beliefs that you are too old to amount to anything into let's try and try again and ultimately produce the exact result you wanted. Failure is a judgment; it's just an opinion that comes from fears that can be eliminated with love. My platform provides an opportunity to begin to learn how to love yourself, love what you do, love others, and love the world. When you have love within you, fear cannot survive. Think of the message in this ancient wisdom: "Fear knocked at the door. Love answered, and no one was there."

I finally listened to my younger self, my invisible companion, my little Eileen urging me to take risks, look fear in the eye and follow my dreams, which is really my intuitive connection in my heart since birth, and I want to invite you on the path to begin your journey of connection to your purpose.

Follow your right brain, your intuition, and listen to how you feel. Have the courage to move ahead, begin again, venture into the unknown, and have complete faith in yourself in the midst of uncertainty. That kind of courage is only accessible when we live from our hearts; it is available only when we are facing our deepest fears. Then you will not have to fear anything or have any regrets in your life. You will never have to experience the agony and regret of asking yourself this question on your deathbed, "Why didn't I have the courage to live a life true to myself and the courage not to live the life others expected of me?"

And never forget...

It all starts with you.

Where have you been called to lead?
What is the *why* behind what you do?

The clinical work that I have been trained to do is satisfying. I help people emotionally and psychologically. But it always felt like something was missing for me. I was unsure of what that might be but knew that I was called to do more. I did not act on this knowledge mainly because my left brain did not muster up the courage that the right brain knew was my destiny. My inner intuitive voice urged me to play the music and dance my own unique dance steps so I would not die with it inside of me, but my left brain was saying, "Wait a minute. Be careful! Do not take risks where you might fail. Remember you are 60 and that means you are in the danger zone. You might not be on this earth much longer." Then my right brain, my invisible companion on my shoulder, my little Eileen, got even louder. The volume got turned up and up to get me to pay attention and to try and help me follow my dream. Listening exclusively to the left brain was turning me into a pretender, and I was struggling because I felt like an imposter, a fraud. But my constant, invisible companion always heard the music and continued tapping me on the shoulder.

The attempts to get my attention took many forms. It took the form of struggles with my own weight, body hatred, and body shaming. It was low level depression and anxiety that was always bubbling below the surface. Usually these struggles, illnesses, and illusions of bad luck finally get your attention, but not always. For me it was Covid! The stillness and isolation of the pandemic along with the lockdown allowed me to connect with my invisible companion, Little Eileen, the part of me that Grandma Mary knew I was destined to be.

The pandemic put so many of us in an existential crisis. Questions such as "What is my purpose in life? What is life all about?" started stirring in so many and in me too! I will never forget the moment I realized that I was being called to do more and that I had a greater purpose. I had a deep sense of awareness about who I was and why I was here. I am not talking about being a mother, daughter, a wife, or even a healer or therapist. I had an awareness of a much bigger question: What is my purpose? Who am I?

My soul was calling to me to fulfill the highest vision of my life, and I realized that it was my duty, my responsibility to help you to know who you are at any age. What do you want your life to look like, feel like, and be like? You see, my gift is to pay attention while connecting to people. I observed that women were longing and desiring a connection. The isolation was unbearable for so many, and they needed to know that they were not alone. As a therapist I hear stories about challenges and adversity in life. I believe in sharing these stories. Life gets better when you share and especially when you share in community. We all want to be seen, heard, and validated. Women want to feel like they matter, that their lives matter. Knowing we matter puts meaning and purpose in our lives. I created a platform, a public platform to empower, give a voice to, educate, sometimes entertain, inspire, and encourage women to believe that they matter.

How have you pivoted, shifted, or expanded in your business in the last few years?

Goodbye bricks and mortar, hello entrepreneur! I have been a psychotherapist for 30 plus years, and I have always worked in an office seeing patients in person. In my younger years when I first completed graduate school, I worked in mental health agencies. Later on I opened up an office, and then most recently (pre-pandemic) my partner and I opened up a center where we had a variety of services, including therapy groups, group meditation, acupuncture, nutritional counseling, as well as employing several other therapists. But when Covid hit, everything stopped. We did not see patients in person for more than two years. Although, it was initially difficult for my patients and me to adjust to the new technology of holding therapy sessions on the computer, the result was positive. I had no idea that changing my routine by not going into my office would actually open up space for me, space to dig deep into my heart and ask myself what I really wanted to do. What is my soul telling me?

I made a difficult decision to close the office. Don't think that was an easy decision for me. I had a partner to consider and an entire center to think about. I know I was being called to create something big and a force greater than myself forced me to step out of my box and out of my comfort zone.

Initially, I thought I just needed to have fun. The work I was doing was exhausting. I was looking for joy and to smile. There wasn't too much smiling during those initial pandemic days. So I started selling lipstick. You heard that right. I went live on Facebook and put on a full face of makeup every day. As vulnerable as that was for me, it taught me several things. I was facing my fear head on. I was terrified to speak into the camera with no makeup on. I felt so vulnerable, but I was having fun. And that was my original intention. I jumped in feeling very exposed and naked, but I did it anyway. OK, OK, you are probably thinking to yourself, a therapist selling makeup? That sounds crazy. Yes, it definitely was out of the box. I am so grateful for leaping into something so out of my comfort zone and completely different from what I had been doing. I moved, made a change, and I became so happy. The live tutorials involved interacting and connecting with women who were desperate to find something to help them feel better each day. They were searching for a connection. Putting on makeup each day modeled self-care and rituals and normalcy all of which regulate our nervous system which was so heightened during that period of uncertainty.

Women were watching! We were all living this lonely and uncertain existence, and I was creating some happiness and normalcy. I had given women hope that there would be a tomorrow and a future in the outside world. I look back to that time, and I think lipstick changed my life, and I smile.

I realized that selling lipstick was not enough for me. As I was transforming and changing during the pandemic, I was being called to do more. My full psychotherapy practice did not stop, but it did not interfere with my newfound passion. I had a vision to get on stage and create a platform for women to share their stories, but I almost did not get on the stage because of self-doubt. What stood in the way of getting on stage? Comparing myself to others. At that moment I wanted to feel like I was above average in delivery, looks, and confidence. I reverted to the fourth grade when I did not get picked for the lead in the school play, and I was devastated. I never tried out for a play again. It is simple. I want validation from others that I am good enough to get the lead and compare myself to the crowd. But we know that comparison is the thief of joy, and I wanted to be happy. I had to remind myself that I am committed to creating a community, and I could not lose sight of what matters. I had to let that ego driven part of me take a back seat. Letting the ego lead you will allow you to take chances and pursue something because you love it. Now, I love to get on stage and feel so natural and confident to share a message. On some level I realize that self-doubt is a natural stage in this process. Self-doubt is a part of doing something difficult that you care deeply about. Self-doubt can crush confidence. So many times throughout my life I gave up on myself before I even attempted because I did not believe in my ability, but this time, I took the leap.

I questioned whether I was smart enough to learn all the new technology required and vital in business. Social media is necessary to a new business to be seen and known. I knew nothing about Instagram and Facebook and algorithms and reels and posts and stories. I learned! By the way, do you know what keeps your brain functioning effectively and keeps it young? It is learning new things. I spent two years learning. I simply decided that I was not going to allow the unknown to deter me from my mission. I realized that I did not have to be perfect. Perfectionism kept me stuck. I used to think everything I did or attempted had to be perfect. I was an A student in school. So I thought that everything I did had to be an A+. I was recently presented with a new idea. I can be a C student and just do it. I would not worry that it is not perfect because that is the root of procrastination and incomplete projects for me. It is that black-and-white thinking (it is an A, or it is a failure) that prevented me from experiencing the joy of many experiences and celebrating myself. My goal and my vision never wavered, but I continued to pivot around it to find out what works best for me. I guess I am still pivoting, but now I view it all as an experiment. If something does not work, it is not a failure. It's just a chance to see what is not working.

What do you want to be remembered for?
What is your ultimate legacy?

Being passionate means taking risks. Are you living life by the book? I was living the life that I thought I should live according to society. I was a professional, a therapist, in the correct clothes, and in a socially appropriate office. But I was acutely aware of that nagging, invisible companion who was saying it looks right but something doesn't feel right. I need more, to be more and help more people in a different way. Am I doing what I came here to do?

Many people wonder how do I know what my heroic mission is? I found my passion in what inspired me the most. As I started to live in an inspired way, I no longer had to ask myself what my purpose was because I was living it.

I noticed that I was feeling so inspired when I was writing and speaking and motivating women as I took the stage. I am inspired as I help women challenge old beliefs such as feeling that they are too old, or feeling it is too late, or feeling inadequate, not smart enough, thin enough, pretty enough, educated enough to connect to joy and purpose. I am inspired when I help women to believe that they are relevant, sexy, and valuable. I am inspired when I help women to become self-reliant, find their voice, and feel empowered and entitled to go after anything that they want. I realize that stepping on a stage, talking to a camera in front of so many has always been my passion since I was a little girl. I am so incredibly satisfied and a bit surprised that I have been able to combine all my years of experience and education, all my personal development along with my passion of performing simultaneously and providing a service to others. Grandma Mary, you knew!

How can people connect with you?

I can be found at eileenlemelman.com and on
Instagram @EileenLemelman

HEALTHY LOVE IS A WAY WE COMMUNICATE BY BEING RESPECTFUL, EMPATHETIC, AND HEART CONNECTED.

by Rachel Levy

CHAPTER 11

HEALTHY LOVE
BY RACHEL LEVY

How did my entire life become devoted to healthy love and the insatiable need to understand and heal relationships that moved me to become an Imago relationship therapist and create a 12-step inspired program for healthy love? How was I called and led to this path and purpose?

Over the past thirty years, it has been my greatest joy and privilege to be a loving safe space, guide, and devoted teacher, serving and making a difference in the lives of hundreds of families, couples, lovers, and many others suffering from broken hearts, disillusionment, disappointment, deep shame, blame, and guilt. Together we make sense of this painful confusion, bringing understanding to it, using the skills of empathy, transformation, active listening, the power to shift, validation, reflection and the five As: awareness, attention, acknowledgment, affection, and appreciation. These teachings are what I call Healthy Love.

You are probably wondering, "What is Healthy Love?" I have been asked this a thousand times! So here's my definition: Healthy Love is a language. Healthy Love is a way we communicate by being respectful, empathetic, and heart connected. It is the way we think based on our beliefs, requiring us to learn about our internal defense system. In time, we learn to challenge our beliefs rooted in a myriad of fears, examining all the barriers we have built that keep us from loving and being loved. And as the Sufi poet, Rumi said, *"Your task is not to seek for love, but merely to seek and find all the barriers within yourself that you have built against it."* Don't we all want Healthy Love?

All our relationship stories begin with our family. We are all born into a struggle. Our struggle shapes us, conditions us, and gives us our unique purpose to fulfill. Our work is to turn our psychological and emotional wounds into our wisdom seeking to become conscious and make sense of our struggle. Our wounds aren't about what happened to us. They are about what we unconsciously made the experience mean about us in a negative way and the decisions we made about them. We are the meaning makers, and healthy love is conscious love bringing understanding and new meaning to our stories.

I was born into their passionate, confusing, and crazy love story, the only child of Danny and Phyllis. I often say I get to teach healthy love because I came from crazy love. We teach what we need to learn. When I was eight years old, my dad, then a traveling salesman, had us pack up and move from our hometown of Santa Monica to Pittsburgh for one year. We lived in a big community, where each apartment building had picnic tables behind them and hills to catch fireflies in a jar in the summer and bobsled on the snow in winter. As the kids played, the parents made meals for sharing on those picnic tables, conversed, laughed, and sometimes drank too much alcohol.

One summer night my father, drunk from too much of his famous hollowed watermelon filled with sangria, went up to shower to clear his head, and one of his tantrums followed. From the second story we heard him screaming "PHYLLLISSS" in his booming voice for my mother. Not knowing why, she immediately ran up and yelling soon followed. After punching a hole in the shower wall, my father went from rage to remorse and pathetically started saying he was sorry as my mother dragged out a suitcase in one more futile attempt to pack and leave. There I was in the middle of their reoccurring drama, begging my mom to stop packing and to listen to how sorry Dad was. I was the self-appointed eight-year-old mediator, pleading for peace between them. My supporting role was cast in the heat of their fire. They were the co-stars in this movie, and I was there to play the supporting role of peacemaker. This is why when people ask, "When did you become a relationship therapist and healthy love teacher," I say, "When I was eight years old, my first couple were my parents!"

It was 1968, the self-help section at the bookstore didn't yet exist, nor did the internet or all the other information highways providing the much-needed understanding of what exactly was happening in my small family. Today with Google, Amazon, TED Talks, podcasts, online webinars, teleconferences, downloadable manuals, books, talks, social media, and memes, I have much greater clarity of all the dynamics that were at play. It is my heart's deepest desire to provide the knowledge and wisdom along with the necessary tools that I have learned along the way to save relationships from the danger and perils of unconsciousness. I know my parents were doing their best at the time with limited awareness of how to be partners and parents and healthy role models. But what could they do? They were emotional children raising a child.

In his youth, my father was an extremely bright, idealistic only child who loved God. He went to temple in Brooklyn, fantasized about becoming a rabbi, but soon became disillusioned. His father was a very nervous, mild-mannered man who played the violin. His mother was childlike and fragile, loved to cook and nurture but later in life became addicted to prescription medications and food. So in his early twenties when my father returned from the navy, he found himself in a caretaking role with way too much responsibility on his shoulders. His grandmother had died, and his childhood home was taken over by his wise guy uncle (the very same uncle my father had been modeling himself after), leaving his parents out on the streets. Angry and disillusioned at the unfairness to his parents, he cut off his uncle and extended family from his heart and vowed that no one would ever do this to him and his family again. This internal rage and bitterness festered into a dark shadow in our lives. This is the struggle I was born into and became the fodder for my healing path.

Growing up in a home with my father's rages and corrupted thinking and my mother's deep-rooted fears, it's no surprise that by the time I was in my early teens I was smoking cigarettes, drinking alcohol, doing drugs, acting slutty, and living a fast-paced life in Los Angeles, an easy place to grow up way too quickly. After all, my parents, the co-stars of my dramatic young life, were cast out of the 1955 movie *Guys and Dolls*. My charming and handsome father with his black hair and blue eyes, fancied himself a Damon Runyon character with his pinky ring, brand new Cadillac, wad of hundred-dollar bills in his pocket, and a Lucky Strike cigarette always lit and dangling in his hand. My mom was the perfect blonde bombshell, his moll. She exuded sexuality and was a cross between Doris Day and Marilyn Monroe, two icons of the '50s, Doris portraying the "look at me I'm Sandra Dee" innocent virgin (cue Olivia Newton-John in *Grease*) and Marilyn, the wanton, unabashed sexual goddess. Together, my parents made quite a striking couple.

I'm sharing their story to illustrate how profoundly our family story shapes us. My mom was raised on the Lower East Side of New York in the Jewish ghetto by a very pious orthodox father, surrounded by an orthodox family and an immigrant mother from Poland. Her mom, my grandmother, had schizophrenia with delusions of talking to her imaginary friends coupled with fits of anger. She would hit herself so as not to take her frustration out on her children. At the age of twelve years old, my mom found herself taking her mother on a bus downtown for shock treatments, while her father was either delivering coal to heat the furnaces or "davening" (praying with the Jewish Bible) at home or a temple. He barely paid attention to his children. She was raised to keep kosher, always traveled with a seder (the Jewish Bible), had a very strong faith in God, and was taught to do mitzvot (good deeds), which became her and our saving grace in life.

Her father kept his tools in the bathtub, forcing my mom to wash in the bathroom sink. Unparented and scared on her first day of junior high school, she stood paralyzed on the steps, unable to enter the school out of shame for what she was wearing. No one was there to take her by the hand, physically or emotionally, to help her through her shame and fear to enter this important door. In her early twenties, she married my father with the promise of a glamorous life, where she would be taken care of, could order anything on the menu, and shop to her heart's content, something very alluring to an uneducated girl raised in poverty.

It was Valentine's Day 1960, and they were married in a temple on the Lower East Side. They drove off heading west to follow the American dream and make a life for themselves in the hills of Hollywood. True to the script of their drama, I was conceived underneath the Hollywood sign. I was born ten months later, the night before the New Year. I have always believed I came into the epic time of the sixties in the state that birthed consciousness, heralding the Aquarian Age with a mission. My mother had always dreamed of having a big family but was given only me. We have always joked that I gave her enough of a challenge to fill her need for ten children, and while I went to school, so did my mother, the eternal student. Together we learned and we grew.

Later, she would take my hand as her inspiration and support to learn all that was left unfinished with me. Although she couldn't answer questions about algebra, history, or economics at the time, she offered me so much about love and life. In what I call "mother wisdom," she would say, "Mother raises daughter, so daughter can raise mother." This has been very true of our relationship. As loving as she was, she was also fearful of everything, needing constant support and hand holding, and yet listened to me without judgment for hours on end. As these early experiences shaped me, this is how I became a natural hand holder, guide, and supporter for others.

In my teens I acted out, becoming very rebellious and destructive. My mother had no idea how to help me, discipline me, or save me from myself other than to love, listen to, and constantly forgive me. Her consistent unconditional love was there in my life, playing a supporting role in my lost years. It is being so lost to myself that led me onto the seeker's path—seeking to know better to get better.

When we know better, we do better. We must seek to know.

During those years when I was lost, I sought love and attention in negative ways without a clue what I was doing. My first sexual experience is a testament to how lost I was and how low my self-esteem was. In junior high, entering eighth grade, after the summer when my braces had come off, and I'd gone through the physical transformation of losing weight and growing out of that awkward stage, I found myself moving up the social ladder and hanging out with two of the most popular girls. Regina was gorgeous and one of the well-known cool sisters whose house was the hangout pad where pot smoking was acceptable to their parents. Desperate to fit in and belong, I found myself hanging out there. In time, one of the baddest boys who was older and on leave from juvenile detention became the object of my attention. He was the talk of this group, so if he was the "it" guy, I, of course, wanted him. So sadly, my first sexual experience took place in the backyard of Regina's home on the grass with a bad boy who I am certain didn't even know or care to know my name. It didn't get better from there as I proceeded to be moved by my parents from one private high school to another, accompanied by their futile attempt to help me through geographical cures.

As I turned 18 years old, this path of self-destruction led me to take myself by the hand to my first transformational seminar in 1978, the *est* training (later to become Landmark Education). My first attempt to get help worked! "Getting It," the power of transformation, completely blew my mind, awakening me to becoming responsible for creating my reality. I quickly became a student of transformation and assisted at The Center in Santa Monica, which fortuitously connected me with those working at the forefront of our human potential movement. My fascination and passion for transformation have been my life's constant factor and focus and the basis for my therapeutic practice.

Why am I sharing all of this with you? Why have I painted this emotional picture of my family background for you?

It is my sincere desire to illustrate how our family stories set us up for the roles we play in our lives, helping you make significant connections with your present reality based on your past. Connecting the dots of our significant relationships and psychological history is essential to fulfilling our purpose in life. Our family stories and childhood stories reveal the conditioning and patterns we act out over and over. These internal conflicts determine the way we approach relationships and intimacy, and ultimately help us understand why we attract the relationships we have or don't have into our life.

If you bring forth what is within you,
What is within you will save you.
If you do not bring forth what is within you,
What is within you can destroy you.
~ Jesus, Saint Thomas Gospel

Using my story as an example and sharing my experience from a very personal place, I want to inspire you to follow this path of personal transformation. It takes courage to get to know yourself intimately to achieve deep-hearted intimacy in your relationships. Emotional maturity is our goal. Emotional maturity requires the willingness to make connections from the present to the past, finishing the unfinished business of meeting our developmental needs in a healthy way. Looking back, we do the necessary work to heal in relationships by connecting the dots of our stories. Emotional maturity is the ability to be emotionally present and openhearted, allowing us to respond to what is happening in the present, free from reacting to the past. As I offer you what I've learned from all my years of devotion to understanding relationships and how to love and be loved, may it support you in finding more of yourself in your stories and their teachings.

The Three Greatest Mysteries
Air to a bird,
Water to a fish,
Man to himself.
~ Hindu Proverb

We are a very elaborate, colorful, and extraordinary puzzle broken into many pieces over our lifetime. Our work is to bring all the pieces together to see the picture of ourselves clearly. Our goal is wholeness. To solve the riddle of ourselves, our life is always supporting us in getting the next piece of our puzzle. Getting each piece for our peace. Every part of us that is denied, rejected, suppressed, and unembraced is called a "shadow." In this grand relationship journey, the relationship between our outer and inner worlds is a vital essential awareness to our ultimate fulfillment. Whatever we are seeking in the outer world, we will find, and must find in our inner world. Whatever we are struggling with outside ourselves is only there to support us in seeing something, some aspect of ourselves that we are internally struggling with that needs healing, in need of love, attention, compassion, care, patience, and integration. When we find ourselves lost, confused, unhappy, depressed, stuck, or frustrated with where we are in our lives, we are actually in the valley of the shadow. This place of mystery, of not knowing ourselves intimately, or being able to see and love ourselves is part of the human experience. Our work is to be committed to healthy love.

What unique formula, framework, or feature do you offer to your community or clients?

I offer the synthesis of transformation, recovery wisdom, shadow work, and Imago relationship therapy called the 4 Pillars, the relational and emotional education for healthy love. Learning that we are *human beings* more than we are *humans doing* is one of the primary understandings of transformation experientially taught to millions of people and me by Werner Erhard in the 1970s. How "we be" precedes what "we do". Working with our "beingness" to become responsible and accountable for the life we are creating, how we show up in relationship with each other, and knowing we are the meaning makers is foundational to my work. Our interpretations, stories, and judgments need to be challenged through self-awareness.

Transformation is the ability to shift our thinking in our consciousness about a negative belief that undermines us or others, and when we shift our thinking, our whole world shifts. Anais Nin says, "We don't see the world as it is; we see it as we are," and the Talmud says, "We don't see things as they are. We see them as we are." Our perspective shapes our reality and our relationships.

When I was thirty-three, my husband was diagnosed with a deadly illness, fearing that if I became a widow, I would need to support myself, I returned to school to become a therapist. While studying for my Master's in Human Relations, I learned from my teacher, Barry Duncan, a pioneer of Solution Focused Therapy, that the solution needed is never as complicated as the problem being presented, a basic solution focused understanding that proved true in my work. By the end of my master's program, Barry had planted the important seed that if I wanted to help more people, I would have to go outside the safety of the box I had been living in for twelve years of 12 Step Recovery.

I believe that everyone is coming to teach us and that every client who comes for healing is also coming to help heal me. This give and take is the very nature of healthy relationships. I have had profound teaching relationships like the one I was blessed to have with Debbie Ford, my first friend in 12 Step Recovery. I became her hand holder, first helping her believe she could return to college, having been a retail entrepreneur and fashion guru, then producing her groundbreaking Shadow Process in Miami. Debbie had moved to California and became the emotional educator at Deepak Chopra's center in La Jolla. She had a genius for redefining the complicated mystical concept of Carl Jung's shadow, making it simple to grasp. In 1997, as Debbie wrote *The Dark Side of the Light Chasers*, again, I found myself in another supporting role. Every night she would read to me what she had written that day. and I would help edit and contribute many of the stories she used to illustrate how to unconceal, own, and embrace the shadow, her three-step process. Many of the stories in her book came from clients I brought to The Shadow Process. As a modern-day missionary, I then left 12 Step Recovery to follow Debbie in her belief that we could heal addiction through shadow work.

Twelve years later, as a successful practicing psychotherapist, and after embracing dozens of my shadows, producing many shadow processes, and guiding countless others through their healing process, I was still fighting with my *wasband*. I refused to work with couples, believing I couldn't be a guide to help them if I couldn't help us. He passed many years later, but gratefully, he was my first love lab partner and my greatest teacher. This led to my next twelve years of study, practice, and teaching to become an Imago relationship therapist based on Harville Hendrix' game changing relationship book *Getting the Love You Want*. His work taught me that communication is the greatest breakdown of relationships based on the faulty belief that we can escape our family history and childhood wounds, especially if we believe we don't have any.

As one of the four pillars of healthy love, Imago theory teaches that our relationships have a hidden agenda. They will frustrate us and become incapable of giving us what we need, and this is known as the power struggle stage. Healthy love can only be cultivated by building the bridge of empathy with conscious dialogue, also known as intentional dialogue, and connecting our present to our past emotionally. The skills of intentional dialogue include our ability to be a clear mirror, accurately reflecting what we hear and validate, seeking to understand and make sense of what our partner is sharing instead of being reactive or defensive, and being able to empathize by imagining how they feel through our ability to feel with them.

I hold every couple and individual I have the privilege to work with in a loving space, offering emotional safety, clear reflections, validation and a way to make sense of their experience. I also guide them to find new ways to view themselves and their relationship.

Then in 2015, I founded the Healthy Love Program. I saw the need to integrate 12 step recovery wisdom with my four pillars with its own 12 steps. In every meeting, I ask each person who shares to introduce themselves by saying, "I am committed to healthy love." I believe aligning our thoughts with our will and our willingness with the belief of affirmation helps transform us. Here, a courageous, committed community comes together to practice and learn the skills of healthy love.

What do you want to be remembered for? What is your ultimate legacy?

My deepest heart's desire is that the Healthy Love Movement becomes a global community of healthy lovers connected to the Nurture Network, which is now being developed to support each other, develop lifelong friendships, and save themselves and their relationships from the perils of pain and unconsciousness. As we cross the bridge into each other's world, my ultimate legacy is to spread even more love.

Come join us!

How can people connect with you?

I can be found at RachelLevyLove.com and on Instagram @RachelLevyLove.

WE ALL HAVE OUR DEFINITIONS
OF WHAT AN ICONIC LIFE
MEANS. SOME MAY THINK
THAT THIS ENTAILS WORLDWIDE
IMPACT IN PHILANTHROPY,
A UNIQUE FASHION STYLE,
OR AN UNDENIABLE TALENT
THAT IS ADMIRED FAR
AND WIDE.

by Sarah Martin

CHAPTER 12

EPIC ICON FORMULA
BY SARAH MARTIN

It is an understatement to say that I have struggled to find the power within myself, the power to step forward into the strength everyone else knew I had.

At the age of seven, I started to question my value as a human being. Before this, though, everything seemed fantastic. My grandparents were racehorse owners, and together we traveled across the US. I rode horses and dually trucks, competed in rodeos, and won prizes. Glitter from my purple cowgirl hat dusted my award-winning pony, Randy Travis. I went on many camping trips and was in Girl Scouts. I biked all around the neighborhood and played in the puddles in the rain. My memories from that time are so vivid and full of joy. It was a utopian childhood until it wasn't.

What I didn't know was that my world was about to crumble. I was about to be handed approximately 25 years of mental anguish that would lead me to self-destructing behavior. This is because while Randy Travis and I were living it up somewhere in the southern belt, my parents' relationship was in a free fall of failure. I was sent away to travel with my grandparents to protect me from the drama. I know this doesn't seem all that bad. My parents shielded me and gave me a picturesque childhood. This, however, isn't the worst part.

My father meant the world to me. He was an avid writer who taught me solitaire and how to shuffle the cards with skill. We would explore trails in the wooded parks, and he would always bring me gifts from his travels as a salesman.

The day came when my parents decided to tell me that their marriage was over. They said they still loved me and none of it was my fault. It was like a scene from any typical '90s movie. We have all seen it. I was crushed, but this isn't where the trauma occurred.

A year later, maybe less, my mother met her future husband. Thirty-three years later, the two are still happily married to this day. While the transition of a stepfather can be difficult, God blessed me with a phenomenal one.

The true trauma occurred when my father made the decision to remove himself from my life. He decided to no longer pick me up for my scheduled visits. He then stopped sending me cards for my birthdays or holidays. After a while, he didn't even call to say hello or check in on me. He just disappeared. It took many months for me to realize that he was never coming back. The hope that I held was torn down by a drawn-out process of realization. This person who I always believed loved me more than anything in the world just left me. He never came back.

I think the question you may ask is what is the big deal? You had your mom and a great stepdad. And don't forget about Randy Travis! The big deal was the question that formed in my mind. "If a father can leave his daughter, what value must she have? How important could she be?"

While my biological father was absent, I found a new formula to determine my value as a person. For the next 25 years, I was led down a path of self-destruction. Was I successful in life? Sure! I placed my value in my grades in high school and received straight As! I placed my value in college and received a full ride. I placed my value in every project I created as an art major, in what the boys in my life thought of me, and later in my work as an event producer. My personal value was dependent on so many activities and accomplishments to the point where I no longer had true value for just being me. I was always chasing the next thing to prove that I was good enough for my dad to have stayed.

I chased this right into burnout, anxiety, stress, alcohol, cigarettes, abusive friendships, opportunistic relationships, an unbalanced lifestyle, and a hollow existence.

Today, I am on the verge of building a $25 million event production agency that is rooted in purpose and passion. I am raising two beautiful and well-balanced children with my husband of 20 years. I have crafted a life I love to live. And I will tell you, you have the power to craft yours beginning right now.

Was it simple? No. It was a challenge. However, it has also been incredibly fun! I have never been happier in my life. I have been able to reach this because I designed my life through a self-developed formula, one much better than my last, I can assure you. Thus far, I have only shared this formula with my close friends and employees. I am here to share it with you now.

I call it the Epic Icon Formula.

How were you able to transform a setback into a setup for success?

The turning point for me was when I was excelling in work. Seems strange, right? I adored my work. It was exhilarating, and everyone told me I was great at my job. I was leading a team and having a blast. What's the big deal, right? The issue was that the job became my identity. The praise I received made me feel useful and valued—the feeling that I had craved since I was seven. My intense focus on work kept me from supporting my family. I was rushing from meeting to kids' dance performances to everywhere that I was told to be. I was never mentally in one place and always thinking about the tasks I had to complete for work. There was no filter and no conservation of my energy. I was on a fast track, letting my obsession with being valued, which I had confused with passion, destroy my life.

Then came a meeting with my executive board of directors where I proposed a partnership that would have lifted a burden from my shoulders, but they said no. After solving any and every challenge that came before the organization, I realized that I would always be in this position. It felt like I was stuck in a rat race, banging my head against the same wall. Yes, I was performing great at my job, but I had no control over my time or what was important to me. I soon became aware that the accolades from work were temporary, and I was on the cusp of losing my entire family. Sounds pretty shitty, right?

It was at that moment that I decided to take a hold of my life. I quit. I quit on a high note when the outside world thought everything was going perfectly. Slowly, I began to reconstruct my life. I did it in a way that gave me real value, value for just being myself.

What unique formula, framework, or feature do you offer to your community?

I was always searching for the perfect formula and routine. I read, questioned, and researched. What do successful fulfilled people do? How do they wake up? What do they eat? When do they exercise? Soon enough, I came to understand that there wasn't one way to live successfully. Everyone has their own ideal way to live life and their own definition of success and of iconic. Merriam Webster defines iconic as follows:

Definition of iconic

1: of, relating to, or having the characteristics of an icon

2 a: widely recognized and well-established

an iconic brand name

b: widely known and acknowledged especially for distinctive excellence

We all have our definitions of what an iconic life means. Some may think that this entails worldwide impact in philanthropy, a unique fashion style, or an undeniable talent that is admired far and wide. In recreating my iconic life, I started to paint the picture of what I imagined it was like to be an icon. For me, it meant strength, confidence, style, and freedom.

Step 1: Define your iconic: Visioning

1. A clear vision of what and who an iconic person would have in their life is the first step. The goal is to explore what iconic looks like for you. Take your time exploring new territories. It doesn't all have to be realistic. Most importantly, do not consider your current limitations.
2. Write down a list of specific visuals, experiences, and qualities of your iconic person.
3. After outlining your icon, write down what you think *is not* iconic. Make sure to include people, things, responsibilities, values, and habits.
4. Reflect on the things you tolerate that don't serve you.

To understand where you are going, you have to know where you started. At my lowest point, I had no objective view of what was going on in my life. I was putting out the next fire with no long-range view or strategy. I felt like I was in a constant state of fight or flight. A key aspect of my growth was to take a deep and honest look at where I was in a variety of areas of my life.

Step 2: Assess Your Current State

The following categories are what I determined to be the main areas of life:

1. Friends/Family/Unresolved Relationships
2. Personal Growth
3. Fitness and Wellness
4. Fun and Recreation
5. Spirituality
6. Romance/Love/Connection
7. Personal Finance
8. Business/Career
9. Physical Environment/Personal Style
10. Give Back/Community Involvement/Contribution

For each category, determine how active you have been by rating yourself on a scale of 1–10.

Write down three to five details to justify each rating. These details should include actions, habits, or tasks—some that are beneficial and some that need improvement. Refer to your vision of an icon for inspiration.

Once you have outlined where you are in the 10 areas of life, it is time to "Cut the Shit." It was in this step that I encountered the most difficulty. I initially felt heartless and selfish, but soon transitioned to a feeling of relief and freedom. I came to terms with my commitment to myself and a life full of joy, a life I deserve to live, and prioritized this over the responsibilities and goals of others. I gave up on the job that fueled every cell of my being and decided to hold on to my husband and my family. I designed my surroundings and set myself up for success.

Step 3: Cut the Shit

To "Cut the Shit" you have to decide and write down in two lists in black and white, what you are going to let go of and what you are going to hold on to.

These lists can include people, companies, habits, addictions, grudges, you name it.

This is the pivotal moment in which you have to decide what is going to support your iconic life design. Face it with strength, determination, honesty, and commitment to yourself.

Visualization is a key tactic I learned in my early twenties when my husband and I placed an offer on our first house. During the consideration process, I started to imagine myself in the house. I watched myself walk down the back hallway and pull sheets out of the linen closet, step into the bedroom, and look out the window. Using the sheets, I then made the bed. I felt each sensation and the emotion elicited. It was only an hour after this visualization that our offer was accepted. I've watched this tactic work for myself and employees on numerous occasions. When a thought, emotion, or desire exists in our mind, we reflect this in our actions. This is why it's important to outline and visualize your perfect day.

Step 4: Design Your Perfect Day

Keeping in mind your assessment created in steps 2 and 3, design your perfect day minute by minute. Time block and describe specific activities, including the time it takes you to brush your teeth, what type of toothbrush it is, and the type of toothpaste and flavor you use. Include the time it takes you to make your coffee and the kind of coffee machine. Write down the type and brand of coffee and the type of coffee cup you drink from (i.e., thin-edged china, heavy, bulky, handmade mug). Include as many small details as possible in your outline.

Explain how each activity makes you feel. Does it make you feel elegant to sip from a thin edge china cup? Does it make you feel warm and special to drink from the mug your child crafted for you? This is a very important part of the process.

For example, in my perfect day, I let go of a traditional alarm clock. The jarring sound makes my waking up stressful. Instead, I designed my waking up to allow myself 5 to 10 minutes to rise using a natural light alarm with birds chirping. This alarm makes me feel calm and peaceful and sets the tone for how I approach the rest of my day.

Fair warning, you may have resistance as I had. To combat this, I identified the words I heard myself say in my resistance and banned them from my vocabulary. This ban on words has even carried through to my companies. My team at Experience Epic Events cracks up at our rule that you cannot use the forbidden words. However, they recognize words are a powerful tool in designing your life.

Should you find yourself in major resistance to drafting your perfect day, listen to the words you are using that are blocking your progress. A few examples of these banned words include:

- Problem - We say challenge.
- Cheap/Expensive - We just say the amount of money or value.
- Hard/Easy - This subjective word can destroy momentum.

Step 5: Execute and Create Momentum

We have just designed a dynamically different day than we normally would experience, but it can't be implemented overnight. To have long-term success with the implementation of the Epic Icon Formula, you have to learn to *enjoy* the journey of creating this iconic life, one in which you derive your inner value, freedom, and joy. Taking each small step and then seeing the results reflect on you is magical.

Let's take one activity from your daily iconic life design and implement it. Back to my coffee cup example. It is time to purchase that coffee cup. Search for one that fits the exact description of your iconic coffee cup. Make it a challenge and compare a variety of cups. Remember, this is exciting!

Now that you have found your iconic coffee cup, you will use that cup with full intention. Be present and feel the emotion you described in step 4. You will do this undisturbed and without any guilt or negative emotion that may arise. Congratulations! You just began your iconic life! This is *the* moment you pick up the proverbial paintbrush and become the artist of your life. Get to understand and absorb your power through this process. Sip from this cup for the next few days or weeks, each time with the same mindset.

Now that you have started the momentum towards building your epic iconic life, pick your next activity to implement and follow the same process. The momentum continues and grows with each step.

It is through this method that I designed my most iconic life. I focused on generating value within myself and removing my self-destructive cycle. Today I look back and realize I have created every moment. From the face products I use to the way I wake up my children, I've designed each part of my amazing day. With this process, I have gained a surge of inner power.

Ensuring Your Success

1. <u>Set the stage</u> - Taken from a great chapter in *Atomic Habits* by James Clear, setting the stage for success is imperative. And

guess what? It takes no extra effort. The difference is your intention and commitment. For example, when you take off your shoes, you can take them off by the couch or where your workout clothes are stored. In all of these situations, you have dealt with your shoes in one way or another. But in one way, you are making your morning workouts easier. This will set the stage for your morning success.

2. <u>5 Senses -</u> When I was running around frantically for my job, I was never present with my senses. As soon as I decided to check in with myself and my senses multiple times a day, my decision-making became so much easier. I became aware of how close I was to total burnout and how my surroundings were impacting my life. I became aware of who I was tolerating and whether they were draining my energy. Once I became aware of my five senses, I became aware of my energy management.

3. <u>Energy Management -</u> The power of energy and where it's applied is a close second to the power of words. Controlling, diverting, and deciding where energy flows can increase my powerful relationships. For me, I've been drawn to those who align with my energy. Becoming aware of my energy usage throughout the day helped me design an ideal day that allows me to be effective and impactful towards my goals and others.

When You Hit the Wall: Because it is coming...trust me

1. <u>The question is not what or how...it's who!</u> I often get caught up on some small detail of a much larger project. I used to obsess over the details, learn about an entirely new industry, and attempt to create a novice solution. This is not only a big mistake but also a confidence crusher. Know your area of passion and genius and stick to it. Next time you hit the wall on a project, ask yourself the following: Who can figure this out? Who has already accomplished something like this in the past?

2. <u>Educate Yourself.</u> Whoever said life doesn't come with an instruction manual has never been to the self-help section of Barnes and Noble. When you hit a wall, educate yourself. Take a moment to educate yourself or hire a coach to teach you how to get to that next level of what you are looking to achieve.

3. <u>Take a Break and Reassess.</u> Sometimes we hit a wall because whatever it is we are trying to accomplish is unknowingly contradicting our epic icon life. When you become resistant towards a goal and it becomes insurmountable, take a break. Step away from the project for a day or so, a week if you must, and then reassess how it all fits into your epic iconic life.

How have you pivoted, shifted, or expanded your business in the last few years?

My business was booming. I had signed my biggest deal yet. My passion and growth were in line and running wild. It felt great! All my efforts were about to reach a lift-off to the next level. Seven days later, the entire world was shut down and my work was deemed illegal. The pandemic nearly erased 93 percent of my business with no respect to any amount of work or effort I put in. I was crushed and completely vulnerable both financially and emotionally. I now understand that I am never fully in control.

After a couple of weeks of forced vacation, lots of wine, and plenty of tears, my need for momentum kicked in. It was time to assess and make the changes needed for the next level. But how could I imagine the next level when everything I worked for was erased? I realized I could operate differently and restart with new methods and practices. My assessment brought out clear deficiencies that I now had time to edit. It became clear that I was again on a path to burnout. For example, I recognized that my health needed to be a priority, and I decided to let go of both alcohol and cigarettes. This decision alone was worth the pandemic's financial toll on my company. I started to input each aspect of my newly designed iconic life.

Today, I am happy to say that I have built my team from two people to eleven, systemized my company, launched two projects, and added another property to our real estate collection. My role as a mother has grown stronger, my family is in a great place, and I could not be more grateful. This setback was a setup for leveling up.

Designing my life to give myself value through my relationships, my care for my body and mind, and my passion is what brought me out of my self-destructive lifestyle. I discovered my value, strength, and impact on the world through giving myself the love and attention that I deserved. I share these tactics with you so that you can become strong in your personal value and control your life in an intentional and aspirational way.

How can people connect with you?

I can be found at TheEpicIcons.com and on
Instagram @Epic_sarah

YOU HAVE PERMISSION
TO CREATE THE LIFE
YOU WANT AND MORE
IMPORTANTLY
ONE YOU DESERVE.

by Stephen Michael McCall

CHAPTER 13

YOUR VOICE UNLOCKS THE IMPOSSIBLE BY STEPHEN MICHAEL MCCALL

Imagine a teenager in a dark room holding a fully loaded gun and staring death in the face. "You have one shot to save your life. If they come, shoot and kill," his father says. Confused, lost, depressed, and a feeling of no hope, he begins switching the gun's safety button on and off. It's the first time he's ever held a deadly weapon. He slowly places the gun to his head and realizes it's his last day on earth.

Have you ever wanted to give up on your dreams? Maybe you didn't feel worthy. Try to put yourself in this kid's shoes. You see, no one understands him because he's different. He blinks his eyes uncontrollably, screams out vulgarities suddenly, jerks his head violently, and barks like a dog simultaneously. Teachers don't understand the reason behind his "bad" behavior. Some even label him as a juvenile delinquent, another statistic waiting to happen. If he told people the truth, that he really could not control his vocal outbursts, who would believe him?

Think back to a time in your life when you may have felt unseen, unheard, or unwanted. Did your voice matter during that moment? Did you have the courage to share your true inner feelings and fears? Or maybe you were like this teenager and put on an Academy Award-winning performance every day to fool people into thinking you were this jovial and perfect person. That is what I did. I was that kid who almost lived the last day on earth.

My journey is complicated but one that I have grown to appreciate. Around the age of nine, I started having uncontrollable body movements called "tics." Some of my tics included both vocal: grunting, clearing throat, barking like a dog; and motor: eye blinking, finger-popping, and head jerking, just to name a few. One evening, I was sitting in my bedroom, and an urge came over me like a sneeze feeling. However, I didn't have to sneeze but instead I had this strong urge to scream out a vulgar word. I was obsessed with that word in my head until I finally shouted it out a few times. And boy, did it feel good. I was so relieved to get that out of my system until I realized my mother heard me. Great, I thought. I'm about to be the main character in a horror film. How would most parents have reacted?

Surprisingly, my mother didn't react, but she responded with love and understanding. She asked me if I was OK and assured me everything would be alright. She acted as if it was normal for a kid to scream out vulgarities. Eventually, I was diagnosed with a neurological disorder called Tourette syndrome. This nervous system condition causes people to have tics, characterized by repeated and sudden twitches, movements, or sounds.

My pre-teen years leading up to high school graduation were unfavorable for someone like me. I was a Black kid with a disability from Detroit that no one (besides my mom and Aunt Brenda) took time to get to know or understand. My grades suffered partly due to being heavily medicated with antipsychotics, which caused me to be drowsy most of the day. Graduating from high school with barely a 2.0 grade point average, being told I wasn't college material, and trying to hide my tics, sent me into a very dark period of suicidal ideations. I needed someone to give me hope, a voice to speak life into what I believed was a dead situation.

A Glimpse of Hope

According to the Centers for Disease Control (CDC), in 2020 suicide was the second leading cause of death in the United States for people between the ages of 10 and 34. Depression is more common in people between the ages of 18 and 25. I remember that night holding the gun wishing someone would help me. It's hard to explain, but a sense of peace came over me almost like a small still voice that gave me hope to live. I dropped the gun on the bed and decided that no matter what people said or thought about me, I was determined to break all barriers and go after my dreams. Think about something that you always wanted to do or accomplish. What was the obstacle that stopped you from achieving your goal? Did you try to find a way around it or did you do like so many and give up? I dreamed of becoming an astronaut, a pilot, and a Broadway actor. My obstacle was Tourette's and giving up was the easy option. So I did the opposite and made it my mission to find a path around the disability. Welcome to the US Air Force, February 1997.

The Power of a Mentor

Growing up without a mentor or coach was challenging, and I didn't have anyone to guide me or offer support when I needed help. So I joined the military to find a community that would welcome me as a friend and treat me like a son. From hiding my noticeable tics and body twitches during bootcamp to my first military assignment at Aviano Air Base, Italy, I survived nearly two years without my true identity being revealed until the Kosovo War started in 1999.

We worked long hours for six days a week because of the war. The lack of sleep and high stress levels exacerbated my tics and made it nearly impossible to control. I decided to take off my mask and present the true Stephen McCall to my military supervisor. I felt myself falling back into that dark tunnel of no hope, and I didn't want to repeat the past. So I chose to ask for help. What would my fate be? Would I receive a dishonorable discharge or worse case, prison for sneaking into the military with a disability? There was no turning back.

The moment arrived, and it was time to use my true voice, one that was very frail, flawed, broken, and defeated from so many years of not being understood. So I told my supervisor the truth about how I got into the military and how the recruiter made me remove my disability from the application. I explained that my tics were out of control from the lack of sleep, and it probably was best if I was discharged from the military. Speaking up and finally not being ashamed of who I am was liberating. I was free to be me. The room was silent as my supervisor walked over to me, gently placed his hand on my shoulder, and said, "Everything is going to be alright." While writing this part of the story, I have tears in my eyes because it was the first time any man seemed to care about me. He spoke life into a dead situation. He told me I was important, special, and needed in the military. The trajectory of my life was immediately transformed, and I was empowered to become somebody great.

Discovery

The next couple of years were surreal. I received Airman of the Year and was awarded a full-ride college scholarship to the number one aviation university in the world. I graduated with almost a 4.0 grade point average which was a shock since I nearly failed high school and received a 12 on the ACT standardized test. Imagine if my supervisor didn't believe in me, where would I be? His voice unlocked the impossible and unleashed a superhero that was hidden inside of me. I discovered my true calling and purpose in life. I, too, would one day use my voice to impact the world, helping people turn the impossible into their reality.

Closed Doors Lead to Great Opportunities

Sometimes we are on top of the world, and everything is perfect, and we feel invincible. Can you recall a time in your life when you woke up with a smile on your face daily and life was going in your favor, but then you received bad news? A door that had been wide open suddenly closed in your face. Maybe you are currently in that place of uncertainty and just had a closed-door experience. How did you respond?

I've had many closed-door experiences in life. However, the one that impacted me the most was in college. It was just three weeks before graduation, and I was preparing to become a Second Lieutenant in the Air Force on December 14, 2002. In late November I received a call to report to my commander's office. My excitement level was off the charts because I knew he had good news for me. When I arrived at his office, he handed me a piece of paper — November 2002, medically discharged from the military effective immediately. I was no longer qualified to serve in the military. Instead of being a commissioned officer in three weeks, I retired my military uniform and became Mr. Stephen McCall. I had a bachelor's degree in hand with no back up plan. How could this closed door turn into the greatest opportunity in my life? I'm glad you asked.

How were you able to transform a setback into a setup for success?

Obstacle - We all face obstacles in life. Some big and others small, but no matter how hard we try to avoid them, one thing is for sure, we all experience setbacks. The medical discharge was the obstacle or a closed door. According to *Psychology Today*, some people see obstacles as a puzzle to solve, while others view an obstacle as a great opportunity to grow. In other instances, people see an obstacle as a threat and confirmation that they cannot succeed. It's important to be aware of how you view a barrier to achieving a goal because it can affect how you react.

Opportunity - Once you accept the obstacle and the associated emotions, open your mind to new alternatives and ideas. John Adams once said, "Every problem is an opportunity in disguise." The overwhelming emotions will begin to subside, so don't give up. Take it one day at a time. But don't wait too long to work on solving the problem. Remember, you may not be able to change the obstacle's outcome, but you can accept it and find a solution to overcome. Consider answering these questions as you prepare to find an alternative.

1. How can this obstacle add value to your life?
2. What are some alternatives to doing what you love?

3. Who can you call for career advice?
4. What are your new goals for the greater opportunity?

Get creative and look for other possibilities. In my case, I contacted my former base commander for career advice. My passion was still in aviation and to be in the Air Force. Three months after graduation, I took my oath of office as a career civilian in the Department of the Air Force. My future was unlocked to a plethora of opportunities.

What unique formula, framework, or feature do you offer to your community or clients?

I have always dreamed big and often so big that it makes people laugh. As the founder of a community called Dig Deep, I offer my clients the following framework to empower them to turn the impossible into reality.

1. **Dream** — "If you can visualize it, if you can dream it, there's some way to do it," said Walt Disney. Imagine and visualize what your dream life looks like. Consider creating a vision board or being bold and doing some of the activities that would be involved in your second chapter. I dreamed of one day becoming a dad, so I went window shopping for kids' clothes and imagined myself as a parent. That is when I had an epiphany. I would have to say goodbye to my shopping sprees on Fifth Avenue in New York City.

2. **Believe** — Why dream if you don't believe it can come true? Consider changing your mindset and believe that your dream isn't impossible but a reality. I've had to block out negative energy especially during the pandemic and sometimes that included family members. I set a goal to become an adoptive dad and although odds were against me, I kept believing. Always remember that everyone may not believe in your ambitious dreams and that's perfectly OK. Why? Because it's not their dream to believe in; it's yours.

3. **Plan** — Like any new business, you must have a plan of action. Outline the steps leading to your next chapter and reward yourself when you achieve a milestone. Be flexible and know that your goals may not go as you planned. Don't beat yourself up if there's a delay in the process or you have to change part of your plan because some things are out of your control. With adoption, I created a budget, outlined milestones, printed my checklist of tasks, and thought I was prepared. When I was asked to consider siblings, two kids were not in my original plan. But I quickly adjusted, and although it was more expensive because my plans were flexible, I was ready to take on the new path.

4. **Inner Circle** — Achieving your wildest dreams requires keeping a lot of the details top secret and for your inner circle only. I would not advise telling everyone in the world about all of your plans. People may mean well but sometimes it's hard for everyone to have the same level of excitement for others' dreams. I wanted to share my excitement with the world that I decided to create a family through international adoption. But after receiving some very discouraging and unsolicited pieces of advice, I quickly learned to only trust my inner circle.

5. **Pursue** — Once you have dreamed, believed, planned, and informed your inner circle about the top-secret plan to reinvent yourself and start the second chapter of your life, it's now show time! You are empowered to pursue and conquer whatever you put your mind to. Stay focused on your dreams and don't let anything stop you. You have permission to create the life you want and more importantly one you deserve. I dreamed of how my second chapter would look and now I'm living it. My impossible is now a reality. I'm a proud single dad by choice raising two boys. I pursued and conquered.

What information can be exchanged across multiple generations?

I have faced great adversity but had the fortitude to overcome it. Every day wasn't easy and at times I wanted to give up. But reminiscing on my life I've gained a lot of wisdom. I believe everyone from all generations can learn something from my experience. I offered these three top qualities to *Authority Magazine* on why I believe I've been able to accomplish so much in life.

Resiliency. Growing up with a disability offered me a unique perspective on life. I was always confronted with a no or "That's impossible," so I had to learn how to push through it. Military boot camp was a training ground that helped me develop more resiliency. Tourette's still affected me daily, so I had to find ways to recover quickly from the difficult conditions of the military. I am grateful for the military helping me become the man I am today, resilient.

Confidence. I didn't have mentors and coaches as a kid who believed in me. My mother thought I could conquer the world and achieve the impossible, but I wasn't confident in my abilities until the military. I struggled to graduate high school, but I made up my mind to have confidence in myself and not listen to the opinions of others. I laugh now at my confidence level when I applied to graduate school. I scored in the bottom 10 percent in the nation and 11 percent in the world. But that didn't stop me from applying. A professor informed me that it was impossible for me to be admitted with those low scores. I ignored their advice and applied anyway. I wrote a letter to the admission's board and asked them to give me a chance and not judge me over a test score. In May 2011, I graduated from the College of William and Mary with highest honors and received my Masters of Education (M.Ed.) degree.

Humility. I grew into the realization that every day is a miracle, which makes it easier to remain humble. I suffered from suicidal ideations as a child, but I chose to put my faith in a higher power, which for me is God. I learned very early in life that without help, I could do nothing on my own. I'm thankful for prayer because tomorrow isn't promised. I remember the day I almost lived the last day on earth and that gives me an awareness to be grateful for every day I wake up. No matter how many accomplishments I achieve, my life will always be a miracle.

What do you want to be remembered for?
What is your ultimate legacy?

It took me decades to realize my purpose in life and to embrace my calling. When I hear my biography being read to audiences before I speak at events, I get goosebumps and teary eyed because it's still very surreal that this is my life. From post-graduate studies at Georgetown University to working for US Senator Elizabeth Warren or the time I met with the vice president of the Republic of Suriname about Tourette syndrome, I'm humbled to have had these experiences. I also had an Off-Broadway debut of my solo show *Dig Deep* that I wrote, performed, and produced. But what I want to be remembered for is being a dad of two.

January 22, 2021, in Bogota, Colombia, I stood in the courtyard of an orphanage anxiously waiting for my future sons. When they finally walked out and I laid my eyes on their fearful but excited faces, I was overwhelmed with emotion. My sons were finally in my arms and the McCall family was established. Since then, we have continued building memories and creating the life we want and deserve. My greatest accomplishment is reinventing myself and starting the second chapter of life as a single dad. During the pandemic when it appeared fatherhood would never become a reality, I wrote a poem to my future sons to encourage myself, and I hope it encourages you too.

"Blind Love"
You don't know my name,
Neither do I know yours
One day soon
I hope we know each other more.

Nervous, anxious, and impatient,
I dream of being your dad.
One thing is for certain,
I am definitely glad.

Paperwork is grueling,
Would I ever be matched?
How can my heart love a stranger,
To one who hasn't attached.

The email arrived,
Would you consider two.
I leaped for joy in hope,
Screaming woo hoo!

When I saw your glowing faces,
My heart was connected.
I sit here and pray,
You'll want to be adopted.

Minute, hour, day, and night,
I wonder when you'll arrive.
While the world fights a pandemic
For my sons, I must survive.

The journey of a single dad,
Definitely not the norm.
But the love I'll give you,
Is like a mother and her newborn.

I'm not perfect,
Nor rich or famous, I must add.
But I promise to be,
Your supporter, your provider, your
Friend, and your loving dad.

Imagine a teenager in a large audience and you are holding their future in your hands. Your voice has the power to change their trajectory from a tragedy to a celebration. Everyone has a story to share and an experience that people need to hear. With an estimated world population of 7.9 billion, if you and I can reach only 1 percent, do you know we would impact 79 million lives? I almost lived the last day on the earth and needed someone like you to share your story that would have given me hope. I think back to the words that came to my head that dark night, and now I realize it was like the voice of my future kids telling me that they loved me and needed me to survive. There is no questioning the fact that you too have been called to speak, lead, and impact the world. I challenge you today to dream, believe, plan, pursue, and conquer. Turn your impossible into reality and then use your voice to unlock the possibilities in others. I did it and so can you.

How can people connect with you?

I can be found at stephenmccall.com and on Instagram @stephen_m_mccall/

I POSSESS THE UNIQUE
ABILITY TO BREATHE LIFE
INTO HUMAN BEINGS BY
SHOWING THEM HOW TO
REGAIN THEIR SENSE OF
PURPOSE AND CREATE
THEIR OWN CONSCIOUS
LIVING, BREATHING LEGACY.

by Kathy Mela

CHAPTER 14

CALLED TO CREATE A CONSCIOUS LEGACY BY KATHY MELA

New Life! Watching a baby being born is one of the most beautiful and glorious experiences. I have had the privilege of bearing witness to thousands of births in my career. Observing this beautiful baby, naked and wet, taking their first breath is truly magical.

Most people expect the birthing experience to be beautiful, wonderful, and somewhat magical. Suddenly, the room fills with so much love as baby girl Samantha enters the world.

But wait! Something isn't right. Samantha isn't crying, and her color is blue. Unfortunately, there is a small percentage of births where babies are born not breathing, and the room is suddenly filled with emergency!

That's where I come in! This beautiful baby born not breathing now needs the help of the neonatal team. This team consists of specialized physicians (neonatologists), advanced practice registered nurses (APRN), registered nurses (RN), and respiratory therapists (RRT).

As an NNP (neonatal nurse practitioner/APRN), an important part of my skill and expertise is to know how to breathe life into this newborn baby. As soon as the emergency call comes in, I spring into action. My focus narrows exclusively to Samantha. In some instances, there is time to ask questions and receive quick, succinct answers to help me understand the back story as to why this baby is in trouble. Not today! Samantha is not breathing, and questions can wait until she is stabilized.

Part of the birthing team includes a baby catcher, an RN trained in how to care for newborns and how to initiate a resuscitation. Upon entering the room where Samantha has been born not breathing, I see that the RN has started breathing for her using an ambu bag and mask. Ambu stands for artificial maneuver breathing unit. This method of artificial ventilation provides positive pressure ventilation (PPV), which is the mechanical action of air being pushed into the airway. When giving PPV through a mask, some air gets into the lungs, and some gets into the stomach. When too much air gets in the stomach, it can compress the lungs and make mask breathing ineffective. Another way to evaluate the effectiveness of mask breathing is to assess heart rate. I take over providing PPV, and the NICU (neonatal intensive care unit) RN who is right behind me moves into action and checks Samantha's heart rate. Her heart rate is at an acceptable level but is starting to decrease. This decrease in heart rate is evidence that Samantha is not responding to the bag and mask method of delivering PPV.

The next step is to secure Samantha's airway in case she needs more invasive treatment in the delivery room. I ask for an ETT, an endotracheal tube. This small tube looks like a narrow straw that will be inserted into her trachea so that PPV and oxygen can be delivered directly into Samantha's lungs.

I stand at the head of the radiant warmer with Samantha's head positioned towards me. The RRT is now present and hands me a laryngoscope. I gently insert the curved metal blade into Samantha's mouth to move her tongue out of the way. This curved blade has a built-in light that lets me see her trachea's small opening. The esophagus and trachea are very close together. I need to be able to see her vocal cords to determine where the trachea is located and then insert the ETT into the correct opening. I slide the tube into place and resume PPV through the tube. We check for correct placement by listening to breath sounds and will confirm with an X-ray later.

Success! Samantha's heart rate is increasing, and we can see that her color is starting to improve. Her oxygen saturation is coming into normal range.

This is just the start of Samantha and her parent's journey in the NICU. While the team stabilizes her for transport to the NICU, I briefly explain to Samantha's parents what has happened and the current plan of care for their daughter. Using layman's terms, I explain that she was born not breathing, that our team has inserted a tube into her airway and that her color and heart rate have normalized with artificial breathing. We are moving her to the NICU where we will stabilize her further by using a ventilator to continue breathing for her and will update them again as soon as we initiate all necessary treatment and have more information about her condition. Samantha's father accompanies us to the NICU.

Here is a small view of a day in the life of an NNP. When I first learned to intubate newborns and premature babies, I often had doubts about whether I would successfully place that small tube into a baby's airway. Sometimes the doubt won. This left me feeling somewhat defeated. Then a neonatologist shared a tip that was a game changer. He suggested that I tell myself, "I am the only one in this room who can put this tube in." I started retraining my brain to believe that I was fully capable and competent to perform this procedure at any given time. During my 25-year career as an NNP, there were times when doubt would start to creep in. As soon as it did, I used this statement and the doubt dissipated.

Halfway through my NNP career, I was offered the director position for our allied health team. As I stepped into leadership, once again I was faced with internal doubt and insecurity as a leader. Although my leadership abilities were visibly strong on the outside, my self-talk kept leading me back to the familiar patterns of striving for perfection and people pleasing.

Choosing to invest time, energy, and money into my personal and professional growth and development turned my life around. It helped me learn to interrupt my familiar patterns and clarify who I am designed and created to be. Living a life on purpose has brought more fulfillment, joy, and balance to my life than I could ever have imagined.

Recently, I have done a deeper dive into what legacy means and how to create a living, breathing, and conscious legacy. Now I get to share with you the fruit of my being called to create a conscious legacy.

Where have you been called to lead? What is the *why* behind what you do?

My career as a nurse and NNP has always centered around love, kindness, and compassion. It's always interesting how we gravitate to like-minded and like-hearted individuals. One of my best friends was a NICU nurse and an NNP. We grew up together in the neonatal world. As young women in our mid-twenties, we learned to care for sick babies. We shared intimate details and our deepest secrets with each other. Rita was one of the few people on this earth to whom I could tell anything without feeling judged. We watched each other's children grow up, and we shared in the triumphs and tragedies of our lives. We traveled together, and we saved babies' lives together.

In 2017, Rita was diagnosed with ovarian cancer. I'll never forget the day she called me and told me of her diagnosis. I got in my car and drove straight to her house to give her a giant hug. I wanted her to know that she was not on this journey alone. In just over seven months from the day she told me, her life on this earth ended. It was a challenging, difficult, heart wrenching time to watch this vibrant, loving, kind, caring, dedicated woman slowly fade away physically.

I have experienced being present for the end-of-life process hundreds of times in my career. I've handed dying babies to their parents to hold; I've held dying babies, held the hands of many dying adults, and sometimes I've been the only one present as life slipped away from an earthly body. We often think that death is a terrible thing in our culture. We don't often like to talk about the topic of death and dying. This is mainly due to the fear we feel when facing our own mortality.

Everyone will have two of the same, yet unique, experiences in their lifetime, however long or short that may be: 1 - We all experience being born and 2 - We will all die and leave our earthly bodies. Death can be a very touching, loving, and meaningful experience. There are many studies as to the negative effects of being a caretaker during the end of life. My experience with supporting Rita, her family, and our friends helped me see the positive aspects of being present near the time of death. It can be filled with deep meaning *if* we approach the process from a place of love.

The week before Rita died, I got the opportunity to be alone with her and share my thoughts. I had been thinking about her legacy and impact and wondered if she had taken time to reflect on her life. I asked her, "Have you given thought to the impact you've had on the world?" She looked at me with a questioning look, and I shared that I had given it a lot of thought. This moment is forever etched in my soul. We talked about her legacy, the impact she had on her husband of 25 years, her two children, grandchildren, her sister, her brother, her parents, and all of her close family and friends. Mostly, I wanted her to think about her impact on the lives of the thousands of babies she had saved. We talked about the parents of these babies and how grateful they are to her and how so many children are alive and thriving in this world because she was there to save their lives.

When she died, I was sad, and I miss her terribly every day. I also know that Rita was not the kind of person who would want anyone wallowing in their shit! Knowing this, I made a conscious decision to honor Rita's life and legacy by making some changes in my life. I decided to create a conscious legacy that involves playing full out in my life every day to the best of my ability, being my best version.

I have been called to lead women leaders (entrepreneurs, professionals) seeking work-life balance. Their biggest problem is that they take care of everyone and everything while constantly putting themselves on the back burner.

My mission in life is to empower women to know their true value, believe in their possibilities, and learn to care for themselves and all they are passionate about without sacrificing their well-being.

What unique formula, framework, or feature do you offer to your community or clients?

For many decades, I was busy creating my legacy without being conscious and aware. I lived my life striving for perfection, trying to please others and almost always putting myself on the back burner. I always knew I wanted my life to have more fun, play, spontaneity, and simplicity. I just didn't know how to add these objectives to my already overloaded and overwhelmed schedule.

In 2010, I joined a network marketing company that put a lot of emphasis on personal and professional growth. Being introduced to the world of growth was a huge eye-opener. The experiences I had gave me insight into the many limiting beliefs that were running my life and more importantly, the awareness that these beliefs could be changed. I could retrain my brain to adopt beliefs, habits, and perceptions that would empower me to live a more powerful, brilliant, and joyful life.

The three important elements of my life had become deeply buried. Through my growth journey I rediscovered my passion for love, kindness, and compassion. I play these elements out every day through the word TEAL. TEAL is my deal.

I live by four main pillars of my life:

Thoughts Become Things

Our minds are so powerful! We rarely think about the power of our mind and often we truly do not give the power of our thoughts more than a passing glance. While science is now in the process of debunking the "we only use 10 percent of our brain" myth, it is important to understand some facts about how our mind works.

The average human has about 70,000 thoughts a day, about 80 percent of those thoughts are negative and about 95 percent of what you are thinking about right now, you already thought about yesterday, and you will think about again tomorrow. Stop! Read that sentence again. We have a lot of thoughts every day. Most of them are negative, and almost all of them we keep thinking about over and over and over again.

In the story about breathing life into Samantha, I shared how my ability to slide that ET tube into a tiny, narrow airway to save the lives of babies started at a lower percentage due to doubt and insecurity. Over time, as I grew my confidence and retrained my brain, my percentage grew from 20–30 percent to closer to 90–95 percent accuracy. That shift happened because I changed the way I was thinking about myself and my abilities.

Everyone Matters

Since I was a little child, I have struggled with feeling unworthy. I now realize I gave my power away at a very early age. We adopt most of our beliefs as children. About half of what we believe as adults started by the time we were four years old. By the time we are eight, we have adopted about 80 percent of our belief system. In response to our beliefs, we start to develop behavior patterns. We take these patterns as "just the way we are" as we grow into adults. We adopt our beliefs and patterns without question long before we can grasp and understand that we do have a choice about how we think, believe, and act. Generally, we are not taught to evaluate our beliefs, perceptions, and patterns to make changes that lead us to healthier ways of being.

Investing my time, energy, and money into personal and professional growth revealed the root of many of my beliefs and patterns was the sense of not being enough. It stems from my perception of unworthiness and scarcity thinking. You may be thinking, "What kind of childhood did she have?"

Actually, I had a pretty good childhood. My parents were loving, kind people who grew up in the Great Depression. They came into parenthood with their own struggles, and they did what most parents do. They parented from their own belief systems, their own struggles and limiting beliefs. Much of my not good enough mindset came from my experience with teasing. As a young girl, I didn't understand it was the love language of many men, including my father. I took teasing as a way to point out what was wrong with me, so I began focusing on striving for perfection. If I were perfect, then I would be loved. Even now, writing this seems counterintuitive, yet it is my truth. Feelings don't always make sense. I did give my power away as a child because I thought the way to be seen, heard, and loved was to be perfect. I became a selfless people-pleaser, intently focused on striving for perfection.

When I learned how to examine my beliefs and perceptions, a whole new world opened! I took back control of me, my beliefs, my self-talk, and I started peeling back layers of patterns and habits that had me feeling disempowered. I started believing that I mattered.

As I worked through my own stuff and retrained my brain, I began unconditionally loving and accepting myself for who I am and who I've been designed and created to be. This helped me look around at other humans and realize that we all have stuff that can keep us stuck, bring us down, and make us feel unworthy, less than, or not good enough.

It's time to shift that in our world. Everyone is here for a reason even if we cannot see it or understand it. Everyone wants to be seen, heard, and loved. Everyone wants to know they matter. *Everyone does matter!*

All Things Are Possible

Have you ever had an idea to do something different? You were so excited to start a new relationship, a new project, a new job, a new business. Then you shared it with someone, and they said, "Oh, that's impossible!" or "You can't do it that way" or some version of "You can't do it. It's not possible." How did that make you feel?

I believe in possibility. In my teens, I read the book *The Power of Positive Thinking* by Norman Vincent Peale. That book taught me so much about the power of our thoughts. Yet, even with that foundation, there have been times when doubt crept in, and I allowed the beliefs of others to overshadow mine. Being a people-pleaser, I often let my desire to please others block out the light of my dreams and desires.

There was a time when I thought I married the man of my dreams. It happened because once again I gave away my power and allowed the shoulds, supposed tos, and have tos of life to steal my dreams and dictate my choices. I lost my ability to dream and believe in possibilities.

I grew up thinking and believing that as a woman it was important for me to get married and have children. Once again, I thought I should put my husband's needs before mine. I did go to college and become a nurse. Yet I still believed that my career (and my dreams) were secondary to pleasing my husband. When our marriage began to fall apart, I thought it was my fault. I believed that I wasn't a good enough wife. Again, this sounds so opposite of what I now believe, but I didn't have the tools and strategies that I gained through the many coaches, mentors, and programs experienced in my growth journey. During this journey, I regained my sense of purpose and belief that all things are possible. My favorite quote is by Audrey Hepburn: "Nothing is impossible. The word itself says I'm possible!"

Lead with Love

As a girl who grew up in the 1960s, I was all about peace and love. I always believed in the power of love. I did, however, stop talking about my belief in love. The world around me started to look harsh, mean, and sometimes cruel. It was hard at that time for me to see how to bring my belief in love into these aspects of life that did not seem congruent. When I became a leader, my heart wanted to lead with love, but often my head led with control, guilt, shame, and intimidation.

After my marriage dissolved, I felt broken, ashamed, and unworthy of love. I built a wall of protection around myself that was made up of anger and bitterness and showed up as control and intimidation. The change began when I learned to unconditionally love and accept myself for who I am and who I have been designed and created to be. I would love to tell you that it happened quickly and easily. It was a process, a journey, a labor of love. There was a great amount of resentment and resistance, followed by painstakingly letting go of limiting beliefs and retraining my brain to accept and love myself unconditionally. This led to creating a more balanced existence filled with radiance, resilience, and rejoicing.

What do you want to be remembered for? What is your ultimate legacy?

The story of breathing life into Samantha is part of my ultimate story of being a dream resuscitator. Throughout my 45-year career in healthcare, I breathed life into thousands of babies through the physical act of PPV. Now I am called to breathe life into dreams with a different type of PPV, passion, power, and vision aligned with true purpose. I want to be remembered for breathing life into human beings by radiating my light of love to empower humans to know their true value and believe in their possibility.

My ultimate legacy is love. For decades, I created my legacy without awareness. Now I get to create my legacy with intention, purpose, and full awareness. As a dream resuscitator and work-life balance whisperer, I possess the unique ability to breathe life into human beings by showing them how to regain their sense of purpose and create their own conscious living, breathing legacy.

This is the way I live my conscious legacy!

How can people connect with you?

I can be found at https://linktr.ee/kathymela.

I DON'T WANT TO BE IN THE BUSINESS OF PLAYING IT SAFE. I WANT TO BE IN THE BUSINESS OF CREATING POSSIBILITIES OF GREATNESS.

by Elena Nikiforia

CHAPTER 15

CALLED TO MAKE A DIFFERENCE
BY ELENA NIKIFORIA

I was sitting alone in the room, trying to find a way to say goodbye. My grandfather passed away suddenly from a heart attack while walking on the street. He was an incredible person and a role model for me. He was so devoted to his family and involved in our lives even if life took us in different directions. Feelings of wholehearted gratitude overwhelmed me. I suddenly saw how much this person did for me—the many times he traveled to visit, attend my activities, and worked hard to give more to his kids and grandchildren. He always called and asked how I was doing, taking me out, making sure I had everything I needed to be healthy, well-dressed, and grow so that I could present myself well and make progress at school. All this attention and care was for me, a careless teen with no purpose in life who spent all my time hanging out with friends and had no aspirations in life. It deeply saddened me that even though my grandfather devoted his life to his family and everything he did was for us, I was wasting it all. In that moment, I felt as if I was a part of a greater design. My life was not insignificant; it was part of some greater whole that started with the first single particle in the universe, and it wasn't going to end with me. I felt a deep and urgent need for change. I was about to make something out of my life, and even if

I didn't know what it would be, something inside me had changed forever.

I kept following the path that had been laid out for me as a child — get good grades in school, find a well-paying and steady job, start a family, and have kids. But deep inside I felt something was missing. I could feel this emptiness that wouldn't go away. Something about this path was not right.

After graduating with a bachelor's degree, I moved back to the city where my parents lived and started searching for the well-paid and steady job. And one day, I was invited to a job interview, and what I found changed my life forever. I sat down in a chair in a room that looked different from most rooms used for job interviews. More people joined me, so I asked myself, "What is happening here?" Then the meeting started and the lady on the stage said things that resonate with me today. She said this job wasn't a regular nine-to-five job. It was a business, and we were going to learn how to help people. The information they were going to share with us would have an impact on people's lives and change their lives forever. I don't know if that happened, but my life changed forever. I felt uplifted, energized, and ready for a job that was not a job but a business I could start with no huge investment. I said, " I would rather live a life on purpose, serving others and doing more good in the world because I have the heart and the intelligence to make a difference." A seed was planted inside of me that found the perfect soil to grow.

Here I am now and for the past 12 years, this is what happened. I graduated with a master's degree from Cornell University and Business Institute in Bulgaria in Entrepreneurship and Finance. I've read 72 books on entrepreneurship and self-development, and I used both of these skills to create websites. I've taken entrepreneurship courses and made multiple attempts to start a business in my free time. I moved to the US believing that everyone who is willing to work has an equal chance at success and that there will always be opportunities in this country. It didn't start as well as I thought it would! The most daring and adventurous thing I have ever done was moving to a new country by myself not knowing anyone. I began working at a job where they wouldn't pay me, and I had to put up with bad managers who tried to undermine my confidence. I worked harder than everyone else because I was afraid I would get fired. I was the stranger. I was struggling to find a home. I spent all of my time trying to figure out a way to get out of the rabbit hole and make a living. I invested in blockchain technologies and did very well in 2013. So I started researching and investing every penny I could save into cryptocurrency companies. I took my money out of the stock market, and my research and gut feelings were rewarded. Blockchain technologies exploded! As I invested early, the returns were insane. One year later, I was about to make almost a million dollars. I realized investing is a brilliant tool and finding the right trends is the most important part of investing. At the same time, something else happened. I became a mother of two kids and fell out of the working world. I felt unhappy about not fulfilling my life's purpose. I was ready to go back to work. I never stopped thinking about what was next in my career and how I could make a difference in the world in my lifetime. With two children who always needed me, motherhood kept me busy, leaving me with little free time. I was burdened with chores and always busy with the kids. This realization motivated me to dig deeper and learn more about what I was curious about and how I could utilize everything I have to create the life of my dreams.

New technologies can genuinely change our lives and provide us with opportunities to improve our lives in many ways. The most important lesson to learn was to gain the knowledge before ever investing or jumping into something new. This was what made me successful. I used the knowledge of my mentors and coaches and everything I read to make intelligent decisions, and this has brought me much success. My mission today is to share my knowledge and help other mothers and women take charge of their financial future. I also want to restore confidence in women that they can work fewer hours and make a positive contribution to the world. I wanted them to know that they can invest wisely to create a better future for themselves, their families, and kids. This gives us freedom and choice. When I became a mom, I realized how much care and resources it took from my parents to raise me. I realized it's up to us to take on that opportunity in life. We must give back that same love and care we received from our parents, and if we try to become better every day, that's how we will create a better world for everyone. Because as Jack Ma says, "If one thing that is not good enough keeps learning every day it will become one great thing at the end!"

I've been searching for a purpose my whole life, and I never found it. It turned out I was living my purpose every day. I am doing every day what I am curious about: learning, reading a book, watching a podcast about business, personal development, reading success stories, acquiring wisdom, and learning about new technologies that help us create a better world and live a sustainable and healthy life. This is what I do every day. I am always curious, and when I sit down and questions about what I want to learn start to flow, I lose track of time. I don't read fiction books. I don't enjoy it, and I easily get bored. Some people are drawn to clothing, design, nutrition, cooking, physics, shoes, sports, human behavior, you name it. We spend our free time on these things, and we don't call it work. We call it interest. Those things pull us in and make us want to know more.

Our obsessions! Everybody has them and we all do what is of interest to us. When I became a mom and used to say I had no job, I was still reading. I was still doing research, and I was still learning and growing. You are doing it too! Our goal is to take these interests and open them up to others to enrich and empower them to create their own experiences. This is how we broaden our horizons. Maybe you love cooking and start a blog to share your amazing recipes. Soon, more people find out about it and cook these recipes at home. That is the greatest reward to see other people being moved by what you have shared with them. What I am passionate about today is sharing what I know about business, mindset, and investing and helping other moms and women to take control of their finances and well-being.

Where have you been called to lead?
What is the *why* behind what you do?

My calling has been the things I am the most curious about, and I can't stop learning. I've been called to dig deeper into things. I feel there is more to it, and there is room for discoveries and breakthroughs because it looks like there is more to it or something doesn't match the rest. As a child I felt strongly about the injustices in the world.

A sense of justice moved me, and I loved to travel and discover. Here I grew up to protect what's right and not succumb to what seems off and unfair in the world. I envision where the future is going. I invest in the good and fight to prevent the bad. Technology can be scary and exciting at the same time. That's why we need to understand what the future holds for us. Technology is becoming so much more complicated than before. There was a point at which I felt I would never be able to understand all of these terminologies and new complex terms. I went to work in a marketing agency, and I had to do websites and thought I won't be able to do that. It is so complicated! I don't have a technical background, but I learned over time. There has never been a more important time for us to want to understand ourselves first, and second, to understand the technology that is playing a predominant role in our lives. Why do we have to understand who we are and the current technology? Social media is affecting our mental health. The numbers bear this out. Many smart people like Simon Sinek are talking about it. Teenage girls have seen an unprecedented surge in anxiety and depression coincident with internet and social media use. A place like the metaverse will have the ability to trap us in an imaginary world that is better than our self-picture, and we cannot undermine its ability to take us away from the reality of our values. We need to have more of these conversations because we are affecting our future.

I heard from the head of a famous venture capital fund that the metaverse is a space for desperation. And it definitely can be if we don't learn how to utilize it and interact with it correctly. We are reengineering the internet and the world to operate more efficiently with blockchain technology, and hopefully this will move us away from the distractions of Web 2 in 3 dimensions of space and time, where we will have opportunities to be part of real life-enhancing platforms and not life-escaping platforms. We can be owners of our data and owners of our content and get to choose how these platforms we use operate.

I believe in the future companies because I see how many more get involved in building companies with better values, encouraging creativity, innovation and self-expression. I see how we can use technology to make the world a better place. I am embracing technology to make a positive difference in the world. What I see for the future is a new generation of companies focused on sustainability, transparency, building a community of creators organized around the same goals, supporting and empowering them to turn useful ideas into reality, creating connected networks, reusables, and generating value and wealth for the ecosystems. And in the next 10 years, 50 percent of the business will be digital. We will possess fewer things. We will spend more time connected to each other and to nature. I see the people in the world as finally prioritizing the important stuff— nature, building smart green cities, working the ground, and going back to our roots with plant-based medicine and well-being. Maybe we must go through this period of technological advancement to become less consumerist and more self-aware. Will we become better humans?

My mission now and forever is to inspire and empower women and moms to look into helping create a better world for the next generation of leaders, our kids, and to preserve our values. We are strong together, and I deeply believe we will accomplish our true destiny. I am part of the change, but I have been called to a life without limits and financial well-being.

All of us feel oppressed being in a job where we're told what to do and our freedom of choice and our creativity is buried. It just doesn't feel right. We deserve better. We feel that something could be done better. I always believed that I would start a business and be able to lead a change of these old values. I believe in individual abilities, and I want people to thrive at their jobs, to feel independent, loved, supported, and encouraged to follow their creativity and their heart. I have worked 22 jobs in 10 years of my life and was trying to start a business on the side. And I've never been happy on these jobs because I have to follow directions and complete mundane tasks. I worked in restaurants, banks, sales, forex products, gym, call centers, hotels, studios, marketing, design, and more. I believe Web 3 will give the power back to talented people and allow co-collaborations, not one executive director taking credit for all the talented work that goes into a project. There is a lot more, but it cannot all be covered in this chapter.

What do you want to be remembered for? What is your ultimate legacy?

In Buddhism there is a principle about the three unwholesome roots. They are delusion, greed, and ill will. We have to be very careful how we use new technology and what values we promote for the future generations since we don't want to be moving unfavorably. Their wholesome opposites are non-delusion or wisdom, generosity, and loving kindness. We should remain grounded in reality and treasure our relationships. I want to do my best to support the companies moving the world towards sustainability, transparency, well-being, protection, creativity, and cooperation. I feel really connected to the purpose of inspiring women and moms to understand Web3—a decentralized internet powered by blockchain—and help them move towards financial well-being. That's why I started a workshop for our Crypto Moms. The future can be bright if we take responsibility and know and understand that we can influence how companies operate and that we have the power to make a change. I want to be remembered for the following:

#1 Belief in self

I was born enthusiastic and full of life, and I didn't want to be a leader or a boss just to do some good in the world. My mom gave me confidence. It started in my childhood and my family's support was always strong. They believed in me. And I carry this with me everywhere I go and in all I do. If your parents made you feel special, you will always feel special and that's something you carry with you throughout your life.

#2 Character

In hard times true character is revealed. How you treat people is very important. All will pass, but what won't be forgotten is how you conducted yourself during times of change. I believe that kindness can change lives, heal wounds, and help others. I want to be someone who is kind, compassionate, and helps others, whether I am remembered for it or not. Thoughtfulness is the most underrated element of knowledge. It's the process of gaining knowledge so that opinions and decisions can more likely be correct. It's about taking time to develop and form opinions. When you master yourself and your mindset, you are going to be good at anything—business, life, sports, parenthood.

#3 Optimism

One of the most important qualities of a great leader is optimism. The enthusiasm about what can be achieved is so uplifting even when you are faced with difficult choices and less than ideal outcomes. People are not motivated or energized by pessimists. I can't tell you enough what a huge difference positive thinking has brought into my life. It turns the tables upside down the moment you view every situation from a different perspective. Optimism is part of your mindset, and when faced with hard decisions or situations, you must make it a priority to view the situation with optimism. It's hard in the beginning but later on your brain will do it automatically. I have faith in a grand design, in universal intelligence and believe that our mission here is bigger than we can see.

#4 Courage

The foundation of business is courage. Risk-taking is essential. Innovation is vital. And true innovation occurs when people dare to pursue their wildest dreams. Fear of failure destroys creativity. I don't allow fear to prevent me from taking a risk. I don't want to be in the business of playing it safe. I want to be in the business of creating possibilities of greatness. If you want greatness, you must pursue it. I am not afraid to go against expectations. I am not afraid of failure. I embrace it because I have no choice. I believe in the ideas I get behind, and they are worth trying. My biggest failures are my grand lessons in life. I have failed in everything I tried, which is important for learning. I failed in business multiple times. I got up, I kept learning, and I failed again. Business and entrepreneurship is testing new ideas and things that have never been done. That's why failure is inevitable. If we know how to do everything, life would be boring. I keep learning and, most important, I keep following mentors who know more than me.

#5 Opportunity

I am an opportunity taker, whatever you want to call it. I love opportunities. I jumped into writing this chapter for the book so fast and easily and took the challenge without overthinking it too much. It turned out to be one amazing experience and my favorite thing already. I found out that I have gathered so much knowledge and insights that I didn't know how to share all of that with people. It's making me feel uplifted and energized, and I am excited for the whole process. I feel that going back into my memories and finding pieces of what brought me to where I am today was an inspirational awakening, and it felt so refreshing! I would never have experienced it if I didn't take the opportunity. You should try writing. I felt empowered by my own story, and it helped me to step into my power.

#6 Curiosity

A deep and abiding curiosity enables the discovery of people and ideas and an awareness of the changing dynamics. The path to innovation also begins with curiosity. And all great endeavors and leaders have kept a child's curiosity as a part of their personality, adjusting them to expand. My curiosity always led to the greatest breakthroughs and ideas. It kept me learning and growing and expanding. My curiosity made me dive deeply into technology and blockchain technologies and try to learn and understand as much as possible about ideas for improving our life. I hope you question everything and try to learn on your own. We can find a way to build on some truths and create better truths over time. My work is always unfinished business, and it's always growing and expanding just like me.

#7 Creative

I am a creative force. I want to create and get into the flow of creating the most beautiful experiences. Yes, every life has good and bad times, but I am grateful for everything that has shaped my creation the way it is—creating our reality, our experiences, and our universe.

#8 Grateful

"Adopt the attitude for gratitude," they say. It will change your life! It has changed my life and when you are in a state of gratitude, you cannot be in a lousy state. Gratitude brings harmony back to our soul. I wake up every day and feel so much gratitude for the life I have because there was a time when I dreamed about it and now I have it. I feel extremely fortunate to live in Florida and am grateful for my family and amazing children! They make me a better person and teach me so many lessons. This was what I once dreamed to have, and I get to live it right now. My heart is full! I take a few minutes every day to express gratitude for my amazing experiences.

#9 Authentic

Be genuine. Be honest. Don't fake anything. In trust and authenticity, we trust in a world where everything is fake! It's the refusal to accept mediocrity. If you believe something can be made better, put in the effort to do it. Be in the business of making things great. And nothing is more important than the quality and integrity of the people and the product of an organization. The company's success depends on high ethical standards for all things big and small. I believe the closer we are to nature, the closer we are to the truth. I believe that the companies in Web 3 will be way more authentic because you can put all of your operations on the blockchain. The customers will be able to track the history of the product from the sourcing of the ingredients to the manufacturing and transportation lines and will be able to judge from a truer perspective when choosing products to buy. We will choose healthier, more sustainable, and ethical products because we deserve the best.

#10 Fairness

Empathy is essential to accessibility and to fairness. People committing honest mistakes deserve second chances. And judging people too harshly generates fear and anxiety, discourages communication, and stunts innovation. I never judge others. I accept them the way they are, and I accept their choices whatever they are because everybody is different. When we judge others or our kids, it is much harder for them to keep up with their morals and the outcome is to lie to protect themselves and be dishonest as they try to escape judgment, calculating the risks. It results in internal distortion in others. All punishment impedes moral thinking. There has to be more for us than domination and control from governments, companies, parents, etc.

#11 Heart and Passion

Living in your true self. Speaking your truth and being passionate about your vision and finding inspiration in the simple things. It's hard for me to do things I don't feel aligned with. My work comes from my soul and heart just as I envisioned it when I was young. I want to leave the world a better place. Being grateful for what I have and haven't even asked for, is a place to be aligned and flow with your heart.

#12 Close to Nature

I say the closer to nature we are, the closer we are to the truth. I believe we will change everything we do and do more sustainably. Web 3 and blockchain technologies are helping to achieve that mission by bringing operations online removing the need for us to make physical products and polluting our environment. It will give us the foundation to build a world based on co-creation and cooperation. In the past years, I replaced almost all of the products I use with sustainable packaging and natural ingredients (there is no need to do laundry with chemicals or clean with toxic chemicals. It turns out oils and plants can do it just amazingly). I started using cleaner food and healing sickness with herbs and plants. And it's unbelievable I am alive and thriving. The body is a self-healing and self-regulating machine. As Dr. Kelly Brogan says in her book, we live in a world where we are showered with electromagnetic pollution from electronic devices and wireless networks that is unnatural to us. We have never experienced that before in the history of humanity. We need to ground ourselves by placing our feet firmly on the ground and allow the earth to calibrate our energy fields. We can practice grounding for 15 minutes each day as a wellness activity. We should take care of ourselves and spend as much time as possible to connect and indulge in nature.

#13 Happy

We are happy to be happy human beings. Work is having a good time and the best mark you want to leave is that life is joyous. The biggest accomplishment is happiness. Follow your heart and do the things that please you.

As a mom, I can say that our mission here is very important and underrated. We are shaping the minds of the next generation of leaders in this world and in the future, and we shall do it well. We shall get the knowledge we need to be able to protect the future and protect the ideas that lead to a better life on this planet for all living things. If I have inspired you to believe in yourself and be curious about how to work on changing the future by leaving behind a better world, we have already won! You are destined for this hugely important role. And you've got this.

How can people connect with you?

I can be found at <u>cryptomoms.io</u> and on Instagram @elenikiforia.

I ABSOLUTELY LOVE SHOWING BUSINESS OWNERS HOW TO USE MARKETING AND MARKETING AUTOMATION TO TELL THEIR STORIES, SO THEY CAN FOCUS THEIR TIME AND ENERGY ON CREATING, BUILDING, SELLING, AND DOING WHAT THEY LOVE MOST.

by Lisa Ray

CHAPTER 16

LIFE IS MADE OF SMALL MOMENTS JUST LIKE THESE BY LISA RAY

It's not that I've always known who I would be. It was just very clear to me from an early age who I wouldn't be. The opportunities for a girl born on a small island in New England in 1972 were limited. The options were slim, in my opinion, and ranged from opportunities such as teaching in a small school or working in an office job for someone else.

I can clearly remember standing in my grandmother's farmhouse kitchen with its large and intricate panes of stained glass encased in thick wood to keep out the winter cold but let in the light. I can remember so vividly the busy scene of workers coming and going, picking vegetables to eat daily all grown on the dairy farm where all items would go inside of her big black cast-iron pots. Magically it was the best meal of your day. "Made with love," she would say while she cooked for her large family of eight. My mother was the only girl and the baby of the lot, so as luck would have it, my sister and I were loved warmly and well by my ever-watchful grandmother, Isabelle.

I can still clearly remember the wooden clothes pins in the woven baskets and watching while she was washing clothes from a steaming pot of laundry water to hang on the line to dry. She called to me, *"Lisa Melanie Ray, you better watch me now because one day you will have to know how to do this for yourself."* I did what she told me. I watched carefully as she pulled the clothespins from her apron, held them two at a time between her lips, and placed one and then the other on opposite ends of the sheets and towels and shirts and dresses she and I hung on the line together out of the small window with glass panes that swung outward.

A still, small voice inside me, more a feeling than a voice, said, "This will not be your life. Your life will be more than hanging clothes on a line." The certainty of that divine assurance got me through many difficult moments during my years growing up. I grabbed a management job early as I could see that it was where I could connect while making the most money. I had just graduated from college and had big choices about the direction I was going to take my career. I learned quickly within that management job how a better understanding of what everyone on the team was supposed to be producing made for a winning team. I started to imagine myself living in big cities and dreaming big. Working to collaborate within a family, community, and schooling while navigating my purpose at times overwhelmed me, and confusion would set in, placing me into a space known to me as freeze. In this space of fright and self-doubt, low level energy festers and no growth can occur. I would fight against the flow of life to create change or situations that I believed were right, ultimately learning it is fruitless to fight the natural flow of life and would become exhausted. I remember moments when I would become still and listen and get curious. These are the moments that I would return to a state of flight and connecting and growing.

I have since taken this experience and created a community and an ebook series to work with others to release them from freeze and fear and return them to sweet flight, where you soar to the highest potential in your lives, families, business, and brands. *Awaken and Achieve: Move Your Life Forward* will change your life and the impact of believing in yourself instead of outdated storylines about moving you and your brand forward.

I didn't want to be a teacher in the conventional sense but always felt compelled to be known for speaking up and inspiring others to seek inner peace and truth and to be more than they thought they could be. I never imagined it would be on TV or as a writer. My first chance arrived when I took to the red carpet in 2017 to interview Hay House authors. Gabby Bernstein was the keynote speaker at the event and had just released her NY bestseller *The Universe Has Your Back*. Brendon Bouchard was on stage speaking from his book *The Motivation Manifesto*, and I was blown away and engaged in the well-thought-out plan to create solutions for their community. Thought-provoking and solution-based conversation around enlightenment and growth and change.

I began seeking opportunities to interview more speakers and leaders and was led to the red carpet with some of the most impactful mindful leadership of today. I had manifested this moment. I knew my path was clear. After interviewing mindful leaders such as Deepak Chopra and Tony Robbins, I could convert these conversations to an inner purpose, unveiling my truth, and in that moment of clarity I was transformed and molded. I could release the old storyline that I held onto out of moments of childhood abandonment that sounded like a broken record. That record went a little like this, "You're not good enough. Therefore you don't deserve love." I had never recognized that this was the inner story I was speaking about until I attended the Tony Robbins UPW 2018 conference in Palm Beach on a media pass. After my interview with him I was asked to attend the conference by his New York PR agent. I went alone and could open my space to learning about myself and creating a moment where I was cracked wide open, and the light came pouring in. In this moment I was able to grapple with the reality that the storyline told to me was not my storyline and therefore I was able to release it and let it go. I forgave myself. And I forgave the person who gave me that storyline. And it was in that moment that I knew that my calling was to speak and lead others who were stuck and unclear and misled to follow a path so that they could awaken to the possibility that their fear, shame, and judgment is what was holding them back in life. When you're willing to define what you are *not*, then what you are becomes very clear. When you see the truth, you cannot unsee it.

In sharing and communicating comes growth. The ultimate collaboration is to find your superpower and then give it away. It is your obligation to get behind your mission and vision and bring this to life for others in your message through your public speaking, writing, and leadership.

I was approached to hold a national pageant title in 2018 supported by STARZ foundation when I worked directly with sustainable housing in steel for solutions to the homeless crises in LA. Working with international brands and charities to further the conversation around sustainability and solutions for housing for our veterans and those with housing scarcity using container homes to alleviate homelessness arose, and I was ignited. I held the title for the state of Florida, went to California and won the US national title in 2019. This brought exposure to a national platform that helped bring awareness to my mission and vision. My speech won first place. I could speak about what I was called there to do, and it was one of the most impactful moments of my life.

When I returned from California, the devastating hurricane of 2019 destroyed lives in the outer Abaco Islands of the Bahamas. I jumped back into action as a producer and mobilized teams to bring sustainable housing solutions by enlisting my production teams with Gemini Media Marketing. I went into overdrive, creating the "One Love Concert," where I collaborated with my contacts, brands like Tesla, Home Depot, and iHeart radio to support, create, and ultimately transform lives. Again, I created solutions and impacted lives with my calling, voice, and leadership, creating solutions for lives to move forward.

Creating that type of impact by using my speaking voice to lead the charge on a national scale made me feel like I was flying. I realized then that we each have a calling. I know that every human being has value and purpose. The real work of our lives is to become aware and awaken to answer our soul's call. It is to grow in spiritual and enlightened ways to give us a voice to speak and be heard, ultimately connecting us all and creating solutions to ongoing issues and insight for moments where we feel blindsided or derailed from our purpose.

Leading with purpose is the reason that something gets done. Therefore, leading with purpose means to inspire, influence, and guide people in your community in a way that is aligned with a group's goal.

Our community at Awaken and Achieve, How to Move Your Life Forward supports that calling and our mission is to hold space for our community to connect in a supported and collaborative and uplifted way. When you lead with purpose in any environment, you radiate an energy and passion for the work. Your passion impacts everyone around you. It inspires and motivates others to find and shine their own inner light. Sometimes we get stuck and mired down in the details. Forget your career. Forget your role as a mother or a wife, caretaker, or husband. Forget how much money you make or how successful you are. If you're struggling with the question "Who am I meant to be?" then take a step back and you can help yourself figure out what really defines you. Although everybody is wired with unique styles, most people have one that dominates. When you engage this pre-wired style, you've got the best shot at fulfilling your potential; when you don't, you can feel stuck. Look to these eight steps to move your life from fright and fight back into flight:

- Learn from the past but don't dwell there
- Year of yes
- Express yourself
- Stop pointing fingers
- Focus on the present
- Disconnect for a while
- Think about the people around you
- Forgive those who wronged you, including yourself
- Make new memories

Looking ahead: It's important for you to provide genuine service in acknowledged ways. By reading this book and seeking deeper understanding of your best life and inner calling, you will know you're headed down the right path. Whether you foster a child, care for an elderly aunt, rescue animals, or support a rock star's career as her personal assistant, look for opportunities where you can help other people or bigger causes. Volunteer work has your name written on it as do many careers: mentoring, customer service, instructing, healing, social work. Don't feel pressured to run the company or lead the project; you may be even more effective as someone's right hand. And you'll likely find working with other people more meaningful than flying solo. Collaboration is where the real work is done. Creating impact within your mission and vision takes a team, a cohesive unit that works towards the same goals. Much like the sustainability in housing projects that came to fruition, the work to unite workers, builders, financiers, and the community has evolved from a group effort. It is the collaborative that creates the impact and ultimately the change you are seeking from within. Remember to ask yourself this question "What am I really made of?" because you will be tested by life.

I remember thinking early on, do I even have a calling? I remember a high school friend's suicide attempt off the side of a 285' span bridge across the Narragansett Bay. I later found out mental illness was at play. I kept wondering if I could or should have done something different. I stopped eating, withdrew, and felt frozen. Just when I thought I would never come out of this deep freeze, a note arrived for me from a wise and loving woman named Carol, my mother's best friend. She had known me my entire life. I guess I just didn't understand that she was really paying attention to who I was. This is what the note said:

> "You are my sunshine, kiddo. I wanted to remind you of something I have had to learn several times over in life actually before it really stuck with me.

> "The good times don't last and neither do the bad times. This too shall pass."

> The lesson, Lisa, is how you stay present in both those times that build your sense of self and character. When we are able to support

our loved ones without losing ourselves in it, we have achieved balance.

Lisa, you could have not done anything different, said or been any other way. Carrie would have still eventually gone to that bridge.

This is her path.
Her story.
Her bad time.

You are a compassionate and empathetic young woman who knows that staying in your own lane will take you far while you are able to comfort others in their bad time.

You are blessed to be blessed. You are highly favored and surrounded by love.

My love, call me if you need me or anything

Love,
Carol

I feel grateful to have been surrounded in my life by community at a young age. Today, I am called to speak with the voice of a woman who was raised in a time when gaming was my Atari, MTV was on, and you knew that your friends were out in the neighborhood because their bikes were stacked in front of the neighbor's house they were visiting. There were no cell phones, filters, cameras, or video recordings of any kind. I find that experience makes me aware that oversharing our personal lives on social media is not for me in this current space and time in the world, and I made a conscious decision not to do that. I choose to share my personal life with my small circle. Staying present in my downtime is precious to me.

My community is small but mighty, and it is a gift I treasure, and I can bring into my platforms. Wisdom and grounded perspectives. Connected within purpose while finding my voice and helping by raising other voices to lead within your own community and create an impact for you and all who uplift you. Taking your life from a frozen stagnant energy into soaring flight and alignment. It is within collaboration that energy flows. If you are isolated or not given an opportunity to learn, you will remain frozen in a space that can trap you. Time moves slowly and at times you're not aware that you're even going through the motions. Everything feels robotic. The reconnection you need to move you from frozen to flight could come from the lyrics of a song, a conversation with an old friend, or a handwritten note that shows up just at the right moment. It is from these small experiences that memories are made and change occurs.

It wasn't long ago that a friend on social media had a new baby. She was concerned and felt the need to defend the name she had chosen for her child. As a mother of three, I let her know that her choices for her child will be many and that she will be judged by all if she publicly shares that part of her life. Let's face it, as any parent knows we walk about under scrutiny for the choices we make for our children, such as college choices, what sport teams they join, whether to tutor the child or not, or whether they should attend summer camps. It can be exhausting.

So let's just be honest. The pandemic was crushing and bountiful at the same time. It was a time to slow down and water the flowers in your garden, be with your tribe, and relearn the roles we play. I think we all began to discern what was real and what was simply FOMO. The fear of missing out drove so many during this time. I look back on my calendar in January of 2020, and there was an in-person event I had been invited to every single day of that month. I had even been invited to two events on the 28th of that month! As events shut down, the sharing and our in-person communication channels slowed down, leaving us all in a space of reflection. Introspection took center stage as we were faced with harder questions and more complex issues. Resources were scarce, and there was a focus on politics, religion, health, and vaccines. I mean, whoa. The mistrust of our media and leaders led to hardships, while marriages, friendships, and business relationships ended. This created moments of fright and deep anguish and made us all harken back to the good old days, the type of deep remembering and longing that comes from your bones.

During that time of introspection, uncertainty, and stagnancy in a world—shut down—I kept remembering Carol's note, *"to stay in my own lane and that I was blessed to be blessed."* So clearly the thoughts of the small community that rallied around my dear friend as she made her way back to wellness, still in a wheelchair but alive, came to me so clearly. She was alive to fight another day. Ebbing like the tide, her bad times rolled away while the good times came in like a high tide on a new moon. Carrie is a guidance counselor for at-risk teens. Her depth and wisdom is key to unlocking potential in these young people. This is the result from a woman so desperate to end her bad time now in her good time, back into flight.

I now know that without a strong team to collaborate, the cycles in your personal and business lives will continue. If you do not take the time to identify and recognize the emotions that trap you in fright, you will ultimately be led to the freeze zone. If you don't work to understand how you can take charge of your life by creating space for new and fresh energy to come into your space, what triggers you and how you react will keep you in a space of freeze and keep you from reaching your ultimate goals.

So much like the young girl in that rural farmhouse who listened for the noon church bells a mile away to chime signaling a midday break for all, I continue to get still and listen. I allow my thoughts to be guided by my inner voice. I am able to connect with my community by lifting others so we all rise. I know you will do the same in your journey to your successful place. My calling to collaborate has led me to speak up and lead the charge, lead my community, while continuing to create a momentum of change that is impactful on a local and global scale.

We're better together. Please reach out.

What role does collaboration have in your current business?

I am a collaborator by choice and by nature really. So all of my platforms are geared towards working as a team. I would not want to do a project without a collaboration because it is within that collaboration where the growth occurs. I am a constant student and a teacher and find joy in watching other people grow and achieve as an individual and a team member.

What do you want to be remembered for? What is your ultimate legacy?

Legacy is not what I do for myself, but what I'm doing for the next generation. There has never been a better time to be a woman in history. I feel my legacy will be clearly defined by the path I am helping to create with other strong women to raise the bar that all are equal. We should all be judged by the strength of our character because in the end nothing else matters but integrity as we work behind the scenes to do the right thing and advance our lives.

How can people connect with you?

I can be found at authorlisaray.com.

NO MATTER THE HARDSHIP,
NO MATTER THE TRIALS,
AND NO MATTER THE SETBACKS,
WE HAVE TO KEEP LOOKING
FORWARD AND KEEP GOING.

by Rachelle Sylvain-Spence

CHAPTER 17

TAKE CHARGE OF YOU
BY RACHELLE SYLVAIN-SPENCE

B orn in New York City and raised in Haiti. I experienced Haiti at its best and most challenging times. I was exposed to the world's best; however, I was always aware of its struggles. This upbringing led me to the dynamic woman I am today. Through my elders' teachings and life experiences, I have learned to face challenges with an open mind, humility, grace, and heart. I have learned not to give up when faced with obstacles but instead to lean heavily on my faith and trust in my abilities and God's mission for me.

I've survived civil unrest, a plane crash, and business failure. Yet not once have I allowed myself to become a victim of my circumstances. Instead, I have grown and become more grounded in myself and my purpose with humility and grace. My upbringing and my parents' teachings have strengthened my drive. Now years later, I'm a successful motivational speaker, author of *mienergi: An inspirational guide to self-discovery and shifting energy*, a web show host of *The Backyard Chat with Rachelle*, a self-discovery coach and a philanthropist founder of the Timoun Lakay Foundation. I've mentored and taught students and women to embrace their challenges as the blueprint of their life's success and increase their productivity by learning to connect with their voice, stand in their truth, and show up authentically.

I was 11 years old and living in Haiti when there was an intense revolution. Angry crowds from the underprivileged assembled in front of homes owned by the privileged. Due to their frustration, they expressed their anger in many ways, including destruction, stealing, and murder. My father's leadership position in the government made our home a target, and we feared the worst. One evening, I experienced a strange feeling and knew I should not stay in my bedroom. I dragged my mattress into my parent's room and refused to go anywhere else. Soon after, large numbers of rocks began to pound at our doors and the windows of the bedroom I had recently left. A single gate made of iron separated us from the angry crowd. Though we made calls to the military, no one came. After hours of agony, the iron gate began to crack under pressure. I was curled under the bathroom sink when the gate lock cracked open in defeat. Just as the crowd began to descend upon our yard, our neighbor, a military man, entered the scene, shooting his gun into the sky, which caused the crowd to disperse, and within a few crucial minutes, we were saved. An assessment of our home after the event showed that the largest number of rocks were thrown into one room. Anyone in this one room would not have survived. That room was mine. That moment taught me the power of intuition.

I was brought up in a life of privilege, but after my father was exiled, everything changed. I was suddenly living in New York, working multiple jobs, attending school, managing a household, and worrying about how long we could remain in our current home. It was a challenging time, and I was humbled. As I worked to put myself through school, I fell in love, got married, and started to raise a family. Since my husband was in school, I was the primary breadwinner for my new family and extended family. Due to circumstances, we still lived under my parent's roof, and I was stressed with life and its responsibilities. My life was not what I thought it would be.

It was easy for me to go through the motions because I was overwhelmed with life's all too familiar burdens. I grew up in a long line of Haitian women who genuinely thought of others before themselves, and I was no different in this regard and followed in those footsteps. Ignoring the very intuition that molded me and led me to safety years ago, I lived my life with my eyes open but spiritually asleep.

A conscious decision was made. I decided I had to live my truth to have the life I wanted. It could be no one else's but my own. I started to focus my energy and decided to shape my destiny. This focus led to our family's relocation to Florida to pursue my destined truth. The decision to move came with its own challenges. We hold all too familiar guilt and its impact on our extended family. The guilt was so powerful that it almost stopped me from moving forward to find my truth and fulfill my dream. I had to wrestle this guilt and push it aside to focus on my wants, needs, and myself. I started by becoming comfortable with saying no. It was then that my personal power started to reveal itself. I began to analyze what I wanted versus what should be. In freeing myself from my guilt, I could give myself the gift of my personal power.

Where have you been called to lead? What is the *why* behind what you do?

Yes, yes, yes, the gift of my personal power! I then started my personal journey to self-discovery, giving myself permission to explore, reveal, release, and reconnect with myself at an intimate level. That experience propelled me to deepen my connection with my purpose and step into the leading role I occupy today as a master igniter.

I've had challenges and obstacles placed on my path, and at times I often felt unfulfilled, uninspired, and unbalanced. I felt as though I was going through the motions of life. I often lay in bed for hours at night unable to sleep because I kept thinking there was much more to life. Yes, I am a mother, wife, daughter, granddaughter, sister, aunt, niece, cousin, mentor, teacher, philanthropist, and so on. All of which I enjoy being but yet my light was dimmed. I was going through life not experiencing life, a feeling that depleted me. I was playing a role in life I thought I should play. Waking up in the morning, I often felt off. I felt like I was missing something. Before I became a coach, social work was my focus. But as much as I loved social work and the positive impact I had on the lives of the people I worked with, I was often disheartened by the limitations of my client's circumstances.

I remember traveling to Miami, Florida, from New York's LaGuardia Airport in December to attend my cousin's college graduation. It was a brutally cold, snowy morning with ice all over the ground. I was excited to see and be with my family while looking forward to the sunshine. As I sat bulked up in my business class seat on Tower Air, patiently waiting to take off, the plane started to taxi on the jetway and picked up speed to take off. I felt the nose of the plane lifting up and just when the remaining body of the plane was about to take off, an indescribable sound was heard. Chairs, doors, and passengers were lifted in the air and looked like projectiles flying in the air. Passengers were screaming, yelling, and an extremely fast plane was sliding on the runway with engines flying off. Needless to say, this was a terrifying experience. I wondered, are we headed to the water? Is that the end for me? God, let your will be done, I exclaimed in full acceptance and acknowledgment of my destiny. The plane stopped short of the water, and we deplaned. I proceeded to assist an elderly passenger. Upon gracefully exiting the plane, I knew then that there was more to my existence, to my calling. My *why* became apparent (a drive to have a positive impact on as many lives was my raison d'être) and the inner knowing that greatness without a doubt was upon me. Since I've been on a quest to connect with my purpose, becoming a social worker was not enough, and self-discovery became my path to unlocking all that resided within me. I recognized that the depth of my *why* lies with the young girls of the world, and later as a mother it deepened with my own two girls.

Self-discovery has taught me a lot about myself. It forced me to dig deep within myself and connect to my core. It caused me to reveal aspects of myself that I never knew existed thus allowing me to revisit stories I held on to as my truth. This process allowed space for me to understand who I was and permitted me to release that which did not serve me. Releasing the negative energies, beliefs, thoughts, interpretations, stories, and assumptions opened my heart to heal from within and gain clarity on what I wanted in life. And only then was I able to start reconnecting with my purpose and understand why it mattered to me.

What life or business lessons have created the most growth for you?

The more I connected with myself, the more I became comfortable and accepted my truth. I took risks and explored opportunities that led me to my entrepreneurial journey. My husband and I ventured into this business that we both thought was aligned with our life's mission of being of service to others and impacting lives. We purchased an existing clinic that was providing urgent care services to the community. We inherited the staff and the patrons. Though we had done due diligence, the clinic never produced what it said on paper. This experience led us to significant financial loss, and in turn, we had to close our doors. Needless to say this had an emotional impact on the team and our family.

You see, a lot of work was placed in building a strong team and trust in the community. Team building and energy shifting became an ongoing practice within the team. After making some significant changes, the staff believed in our mission and worked hard to ensure the clinic's success to no avail. "We are all in it together!" is the motto that has kept my team in sync. This belief catapults them to buy into the practice's mission and vision, understanding that we rise as one and fall as one. Such philosophy enabled the team to work towards success. In turn, it created a sense of trust, safety, and an openness to grow collectively as a community. Communicating clearly and effectively our expectations while keeping all lines and doors open to respectfully sharing opinions and actively listening was extremely important. And by walking my talk, showing up authentically and in full transparency, respecting, celebrating and valuing each member as an incremental part of the team while instilling the importance of celebrating all wins (small or big) was imperative. This has helped me build and keep my team committed, motivated, and empowered with high morals and integrity.

After countless sleepless nights, stuck in the unknown, borrowing from Peter to pay Paul, there were no other options but to cut our losses. This was one of the toughest decisions I have had to make, and I relied heavily on my faith to carry me through. I learned to fully surrender to the highest power and allow his will to be made. I learned to accept that I cannot control and trust that there's a greater purpose.

Well, my self-discovery journey prepared me to handle such setbacks with humility and grace. It afforded me the tools to be patient with myself, trust, and practice understanding. As I had mentioned earlier, service and impact are my life's purpose. Lo and behold I was placed in this circumstance to do just that. I am often reminded of this quote by Marilyn Monroe that says, "Good things fall apart so that better things can fall together." Upon closing our doors at least three staff members remained working with me for an entire year without pay helping me build my current practice. I attributed their decision to the positive impact I had on their lives and career trajectory. This right there was my paycheck! I instantly was appreciative of the setback because within it all I was living my purpose out loud: *impacting lives*!

Dumbfounded by the outpouring support, I leaned in, gave thanks, and pooled the lessons from the experiences. So many things have gone right in the midst of it all. I recognized the strength of my marriage and my family, acknowledged how grounded I was spiritually and in my faith, and noticed how impactful I am in servicing others. Without a doubt, I ignited their inner motivations to take charge of their lives and create change. I automatically embraced the setback as an opportunity, with the strong belief that there are no problems, only solutions. I am always reminded that "Life is always happening for us not to us." —Tony Robbins

Acceptance is one of the key pieces of my personal and professional growth process. Learning to accept that we are born with purpose and that the creator's or the universe's plans are uniquely designed for each of us has been a turning point in my life. It provided me the foresight to navigate life and its challenges with an open mind and heart. I accepted challenges as part of the journey, and this gave me the strength to face and push through any challenge with grace and humility. Acceptance is freeing; it opens the doors to self-love and self-confidence.

Yes, it is an incredible sensation to have, owning who you are and accepting your truth. As I wrote in my book *minergi*, "Your **truth** is what makes you real, rare, and fully *authentic*. Your **values** define you. Your characteristics paint you. Your gifts express you, and your story is unique to you. None of these can be duplicated. In this quest of self-acceptance, we acquaint ourselves with ourselves, giving birth to a new level of self-intimacy. We identify all that makes us happy or sad, what brings us overall joy, or what generates dissatisfaction. We gain clarity about our likes and dislikes, leading to the understanding that these feelings or triggers are the pure essence of who we are at the core."

During my journey I fully submerged myself in identifying my values, understanding my characteristics, appreciating my gifts, and more so, accepting my history as I proceeded to create my new story. I traveled, read, studied, wrote, and explored. It was without fail the best experience I've ever had. I found a depth of love, respect, and understanding of myself, allowing me to forgive myself and accept myself as I am without reservation. I began to understand that my experiences (good, bad, and ugly) were part of my history, which contributed to who I had become and yet they did not define me. When you practice unconditional self-acceptance, you can begin to love yourself, embrace your authentic self, and work on improving your less than desirable traits and qualities. "Full acceptance can lay the foundation for positive self-esteem, and the two frequently go hand in hand, but they concern two different aspects of how we think and feel about ourselves." —mienergi

How were you able to transform a setback into a setup for success?

What I know to be true is that my life's lessons have set me up for personal and professional success. Each setback set me up, and I experienced transformation in each area of my life that needed to be refined and strengthened. My authenticity has set me apart in every aspect of my life by establishing a culture of trust, honesty, positivity, and service. As the master igniter, when I speak, I come from a place of truth and authenticity, I light that fire within my listeners to take positive action in their lives to create change. That unique skill is what has helped me build my reputation within my market. I believe that one's authenticity speaks to who they are, what they want, and why it matters to them. It, in turn, allows for full transparency in all aspects of life. I am now on a mission to impact women and young girls globally to own their voices, stand in their truth, and show up authentically.

Taking charge of yourself requires you to connect with that light that resides within and build strength and confidence through the process of self-discovery:

First, unmask your realness by revealing who you are, releasing what does not serve, and reconnecting with your truth.

Second, shift your energy by breaking through self-resistance, facing adversity with clarity of mind, and building strength to push through with openness of heart.

Third, see yourself as you are by becoming more self-aware and practicing self-acceptance and self-love.

Only then can you start to create change in your life, the change you've been yearning to have, to build the life that fulfills you, one that is filled with abundance in every area. This is the change that will set you apart and open the doors to your greatness. That change will require you to execute and be accountable to these four keys:

- Make a **Decision**
- **Commit** to it
- Be **Consistent**
- Be **Disciplined**

Make a decision that you want to create change in your life. What does your vision look or feel like? Once clear, create a plan with specific measurable and attainable goals. Then remain consistent by having an accountability system or a partner. And discipline yourself with a structured approach that is aligned with your values and daily routines.

What do you want to be remembered for?
What is your ultimate legacy?

As I reflect on my life's journey and experiences, I know that I have been placed in each situation with a purpose and for a purpose that is greater than myself. And there's no other option but to keep going. No matter the hardship, no matter the trials, and no matter the setbacks, we have to keep looking forward and keep going. Each experience provides me with the tools to keep going. Now when I am faced with a setback, I gracefully say to myself that I'm about to grow. I am a strong believer in the saying "What doesn't break you makes you." The more I connect with myself I become more planted in my purpose, giving me the voice to share and impact lives.

My legacy is to create a global forum where I impact and lead girls and women to find power in owning their voices, embracing their truth by standing tall and proud and not being ashamed to show up for themselves proud and authentically. On my tombstone I will be remembered for positively impacting and empowering many with hope and inspiration and motivating them to take action in their lives. My trust and faith in knowing that God has my back keeps me going. He created us with purpose, and it is our responsibility in this lifetime to connect with this purpose. Now there's no stopping me!

"Don't sit on your intentions, act on them!"

Rachelle

How can people connect with you?

I can be found at rachellesylvain.com and on Instagram @_rachellesylvain.

I BELIEVE THAT WHEN
WE CAN COME TOGETHER,
WE CAN ALL BRING OUR
UNIQUE GIFTS AND SUPPORT
ONE ANOTHER IN A MUCH
BETTER WAY THAN WHEN
WE WORK INDIVIDUALLY.

by Bhavna Srivastava

CHAPTER 18

ACCEPTING MY CALLING
BY BHAVNA SRIVASTAVA

On October 2nd, 2005 after my near-death experience being in a car accident and being saved by God, I started my journey. Initially, it was difficult to understand that God came to save me and my life and that I was important when people forgot about me.

What hurt most was that I was always there for my community and yet nobody showed up or even asked how I was doing. But I was comforted, knowing that I was very important to God and that he had not forgotten about me even though I did not remember him every day. From that point in my life, I vowed to remember him and thank him every morning for my life since I'm alive and here because of him.

During this journey, I was shown what my purpose was when I was still going through the trauma of that accident. I was in a lot of pain. My entire body hurt: my back, neck, shoulders, and I could go on and on. I have always been there for everyone, and I will never change that. Now, only God was there for me. Wow! It was a great feeling, and I also felt at peace. I was no more alone as this was a new country for me.

Have you ever felt that you put everyone's need ahead of yours and are always last on the list? I did that for many years. That accident changed that, and it was a hard lesson for me to start putting myself first. Did it happen overnight? No, not at all. I still struggled to put everyone first, but you know what changed was I was in a lot of physical pain in my body 24/7.

Due to the car accident, I had internal pain in my legs all the time, and there were times when I could not even walk or move. I went to all the physical therapy places and worked with many people trying to get better and even tried water physical therapy, but nothing worked. The pain would be gone for a few minutes here and there but still came back. Imagine living with it all the time.

After some time, it started to get to me and got me irritated and sad, and I began to feel no light. Remember, I was still connected to God and started to talk to him even more. I was taking regular ibuprofen 800 mg or more sometimes. Slowly, I thought of trying alternative therapy, like massage. That did help for some time more than the ibuprofen, but it did not completely go away. I was so exhausted from trying everything, and now I was living with pain all the time.

During this time, I was still talking to God but never asked him to take away the pain as I felt I shouldn't ask for anything for myself. Does that sound familiar? As givers, we always give but never ask anyone for anything for ourselves.

On March 7th, 2007, God showed me a humongous vision and told me that this was my purpose, and I had to create it. I froze and got scared as I did not even know how to do anything as I was not a businesswoman and I told him that. He said, "Don't worry. You start and do as I say, and I will bring you my people." Well, in April of 2012, I finally said yes to him. So after procrastinating for three years, I agreed to start work on the vision he showed me. That day when I went in to hand in my resignation in the morning, I walked into the building in pain and limping and came out without a limp. All my pains had disappeared. A miracle happened. I understood from that day that when you hear your calling, God begins to help in your life with everything.

I just rented a room. I never did any marketing, but people just started to come, and I started to heal people. At that time, I just knew reiki, so I began to practice that. During that year itself, I was asked to hold a Golden Light Retreat for a day on December 21st, unaware of what it would be and why I had to do it. But by this time, I had just started to believe and trust in God and said yes to everything he asked me to do.

Where have you been called to lead?
What is the *why* behind what you do?

I have been called as a leader to create communities of like-minded people to live in a sacred space in my golden light, which is living under the protection of unconditional love light, which helps them to create the golden age and live in the 5D world. This will help them to be who they are at the soul level and shine their light all the time.

When I asked God "Why me?" he replied, "Why not you?" He also reminded me of how he had pulled me out of the feelings of sadness, hopelessness, feeling lost, living in pain, and so much more. He had asked me if I wanted to do the same for others. I knew how it would feel for them and how it would change their lives, so I said yes from that day. I never said no to him but always asked him to explain as I always wanted to know more. I finally asked him to be my teacher, and he said yes to me. That was the most significant day for me. My big why is my promise to God to help those who need help and feel alone and create the golden age to spread love and peace in the world. Sometimes, without us even realizing it our why becomes bigger than our lives and our lives change as we start to shift others.

When you accept to walk in your purpose, things begin to align, and the struggles you go through start to diminish, but if you procrastinate in accepting your calling, you get stuck in a pattern. This pattern can be anything, like receiving pain, hurt from relationships, physical body pain, or sickness. During my journey of healing, coaching, and mentoring people, I have seen how quickly shifts happen and people create miracles when they accepted their calling.

I struggled with physical body pain when I kept procrastinating about being the Golden Light and pushed away my purpose. The day I accepted it completely, things felt so much easier.

Initially, I would have people come to my house when the doctors gave them little time to live, and I would ask God what I should do, and he would say you know what to do, and I would do something, and they are still alive. Very powerful and very humbling for me as days went by. In 2012 the whole universe came together to prepare me for the 21st of December. I was in for a surprise. We got comfortable that everything was going well, but God always has a surprise for us. In September, I was shown a movie about all my lifetimes, and I was told that I'm the oldest living soul in the entire universe, not just Earth. Knowing your purpose brings with it responsibilities. I was about to freeze again but had a more powerful spiritual awakening and as a result I started to connect and see and feel everyone's pain.

What unique formula, framework, or feature do you offer your community or clients?

On December 21st, 2012, at 11.30 p.m., I awakened to who I am and became the Golden Light and from then started the unique journey of healing people with the Golden Light. Since 2019 I have taught people to be Golden Light healers and practitioners. Golden Light healers take two full days to learn how to heal themselves and others and receive certificates for levels 1 and 2. Whereas a Golden Light practitioner is on a seven-year journey. Each year, they get closer to becoming fully enlightened and understanding that they are ambassadors of love and peace in the world.

How have you pivoted, shifted, or expanded your business in the last few years?

We all start our lives believing in doing better, living better, and being there for our families. Well, this journey shifted my life 180 degrees when I said yes to my calling and accepted I was the Golden Light.

I opened my holistic wellness center (Bhavna's Wellness Group) with zero dollars, not knowing how and what I would be doing, but I trusted God completely. Miracles started to happen for people who came, and transformation started in the lives of 50,000+ people who visited my center or our events in person, via Zoom, expos, fairs, workshops, and retreats from 2008 until the present. We've received many awards locally and internationally, and in the process, I became an international speaker, bestselling author of two books, certified coach, mentor, trainer, and much more so I could help and serve more people. I also now specialize in trauma and guiding and transforming people's lives to help shine their lights in the world.

What information can be exchanged across multiple generations?

Every old soul comes here with a purpose. Sometimes, when you don't hear your calling or feel confused and keep ignoring it, then it hurts you more than others. That's why it's so important to connect to an older soul, who is older than you at soul level, and ask for guidance in your soul's journey so you can move forward, but you have to accept your calling. In order to do that first, you have to forgive all those who have hurt you and let go of the pain. Know that to move forward, you have to understand your pain to feel the pain of others, but your pain must not become your weakness but your strength. Teach your kids how to love and connect with each other, communicate, talk, laugh, forgive, and be peaceful. Loving yourself and others is very important, and it's important for all generations, whether it's the older generation or those aged 30–65, and even the younger generation should live these thoughts, values, and principles. This helps create a better you and a better world, as the ripple effect you create is going to be bigger than you can even imagine. I always say, "In vulnerability lies your strength."

How were you able to transform a setback into a setup for success?

I always believe that one must keep on working and doing your best and leave the rest to God. And when you do your best, you will never regret anything in life, whether your employees, clients, friends, or anyone else betrays you. When you focus your attention on the service aspect of just giving and making sure you do not bring your ego into it, things will always be OK. I have had moments when people stole my intellectual property, my style, my clients, but I kept believing in my calling and that what is mine is mine, and nobody can take that away from me. I kept moving forward with that truth and kept transforming lives. Life is very unpredictable; sometimes your own people can hurt and betray you, but if you believe and have accepted your calling and continue your work, nobody can take away that calling. I believe the vision shown to me by God is mine. If he wanted someone else to have it, they would have seen it too. If they did, then maybe, you are supposed to work together; otherwise just focus on your service and keep on walking steadily and slowly, and one day, you will be sprinting. It is simple and keeps life simple. Don't complicate things in life. Love is simple and so is God. Loving him is the simplest of all, but we are never taught how to make it simple, so we are always very confused and lost about everything, which is why complications happen. So just be simple, keep moving forward, and keep doing your work with his trust in you.

What role does collaboration have in your current business?

My business is a collaboration of all like-minded holistic and spiritual people. I have a wellness center in a physical location. Collaboration is the most important aspect of my business as I believe that when we can come together, we can all bring our unique gifts and support one another in a much better way than when we work individually.

What life or business lessons have created the most growth for you?

To trust your inner guidance, your inner knowing, and to always stay connected was one of the biggest lessons I had to grow with every day. The hardest one was when sometimes the mind would try to control and ask are you sure this is OK or right? Also to keep trusting people even though sometimes they would cheat me and use me and not pay for the classes or sessions. I still trust them but have become smart, so they cannot cheat or fool me again. I am still able to genuinely transform others. Protection is very important for all healers or sensitive people. You must protect your energy field, aura, your mind, your family, your home and your physical body. Those who haven't done this have actually fallen very sick.

What do you want to be remembered for? What is your ultimate legacy?

My ultimate legacy is to create the golden age, which is where people live with love and peace. They are happy with each other and live as a brotherhood and sisterhood. They are kind, loving, and have compassion for each other. It is also about stepping into your daring and courage, and finally getting to those things you've been wanting and dreaming of accomplishing, despite any lingering fears. It is also about recognizing your soul, its light, and your calling, and living with the calling every day filled with compassion and being happy that you are living every moment of your life to the fullest and always dreaming big. Always believe and trust each other and just love each other. This is where our future generations will always be together and so it is.

I believe in passing on knowledge with love:

"Love with your heart and soul always."
"Live every day fully."
"Live every moment and cherish that memory forever."
"Never quit on the people you love."
"Just be there."

How can people connect with you?

I can be found at <u>Bhavnasrivastava@bhwellnessgroup.com</u> and on Facebook @BHWellnessGroup.

MY PASSION IS SHOWING
YOU HOW TO WAKE UP THE
CONTROL YOU ARE CAPABLE
OF TO MAKE CHANGES FOR
A BETTER LIFE THROUGH
THE IMAGINATIVE
HORSEPOWER OF
YOUR BRAIN.

by Lori Blum Sugarman

CHAPTER 19

WHY QUACK LIKE A DUCK WHEN YOU CAN ROAR LIKE A LION
BY LORI BLUM SUGARMAN

"No, I won't make you quack like a duck!" I say during a question and answer forum around clinical hypnotherapy. "Unless you tell me that's what you want."

"I am not letting someone else control my mind," another brave guest shouts out.

"Smart thinking!" I say, "because you never should, but here's a secret. Hypnotherapy helps you gain back control over anything."

I am a clinical hypnotherapist and have been in practice since 2007. My expertise is guiding people into a blissful state of relaxation so the brain can do its work naturally. To be entrusted to help children, teens, and adults overcome moderate to crippling attitudes, beliefs, and habits that prevent peace of mind, emotional happiness, or achievement of desired outcomes is the most rewarding partnership imaginable. I am deeply humbled to join together with my clients and be a positive agent for change.

The courage to try something often surrounded by myth and general misunderstanding is admirable. *The human brain is a miraculous organ capable of transformational change in a relatively short period of time, and that's just the fact of the brain's capability to change.* I don't consider myself to be one to hypnotize people. I consider myself to be one who de-hypnotizes people.

My mother was wise, but a screamer and a yeller. I share part of her story for parents who may be raising teenagers—those moody hormonal beings who are dealing with much more than we know—and to share my mom's wisdom. Raising five kids who came in six years from oldest (me) to youngest, I give her screeching vocal talent a pass. My dad was home only on the weekends due to working in a six-state territory. Our mom knew how to keep problems small by not giving them a lot of attention. When my brother David threatened to run away from home, she offered to help him pack. He did run... right into a tree, so it was a short-lived escape. I once confided to her that a third-grade boy was calling me names. She asked me if I was a man or a mouse and then walked away. I was going to get married at 17, the day after my high school graduation. With the wedding guest list in hand, I announced to my mother I was getting married in two months' time (August). My boyfriend of three years had dropped out of high school and was set to inherit his father's junkyard business. I was in love and ready to break away from a rambunctious household of seven people. After my proclamation, in a calm voice as if I had said I'm going to take a walk, Mom said, "You know what, Lori? Go to Guilford College for one semester. You'll turn 18 in January, and then if you still want to get married, you'll have our blessings." Had she made an issue, I would have eloped. She was calm, logical, and it was reasonable, so I agreed. August came and I moved into Binford Dorm at Guilford College. The world opened up. New friendships with students from different nationalities, religions, and life experiences were exhilarating. The door to marriage at 17 was closed. It was my first impactful lesson on the power of suggestion, which is the basis of hypnosis—communicating in a relaxed state that does not invoke anxiety, anger, or trigger a defensive response.

Guilford College stirred me with intrigue, witnessing different belief systems. I also observed the mind's fragility with several friends I had made. One friend streaked (a running naked phase in the '70s) through the cafeteria in his underwear due to tremendous stress knowing his family was in war-torn Uganda. Another girl went into a mental breakdown after a breakup from her college love. A normal girl I'd just recently spent time with was carted away by the white funny farm truck due to her hallucinatory experiences.

In my first semester I volunteered to be a biofeedback lab rat. Electrodes attached to my head measured brain waves as I thought myself into another place, which was the ocean, laying on the sand, bathed in warm golden sunlight, feeling the ever-present breeze, hearing the waves roar up and fizzle out at the shoreline along with the seagull calls. To completely lose track of the present by imagining myself at the ocean was an act of self-hypnosis. I used it 40 years later to have a colonoscopy without anesthesia. Little did I know a wrong turn, and a huge roadblock moving from one state to another would take me into the world of hypnotherapy.

What life lessons have created the most growth for you?

It seems I was always falling in love. My new love at Guilford was a senior, and after he graduated, I no longer wanted to be at Guilford without him, so I transferred to UNC-G sophomore year, second semester. In April a sign on the wall caught my attention.

WANTED: STUDENTS WHO CAN TRAVEL, TALK TO PEOPLE, AND WANT TO EARN 2500.00 THIS SUMMER.

It sounded right up my alley, so I attended a two-hour lecture by a baby-faced junior, who became a lifelong dear friend and within two years, married my best friend. At 19 years old, I determined if Paul Dixon could make $2500.00 selling Bible reference books door to door, then so could I. Two hours later, I signed a contract with the Southwestern Company, a contract I would also provide to those I recruited the subsequent four years after my first summer of selling Bible reference books, a cookbook, and a set of children's books door to door during my six-day 75-hour work week. All student salesmen went to Nashville, Tennessee for a week of positivity and sales training, where we were convinced to make 30 demos a day, appreciate rejection because it meant a yes was around the corner, knock on the door of the first house at 8:00 a.m. and the last house at 8:30 p.m. six days a week, take cold showers in the morning, and sing the "It's a Great Day to be a Bookman" song daily.

Guest speakers during our training included Zig Ziglar. Our training material contained *The Greatest Salesman in the World*, by Og Mandino. The belief in self, working hard, and not quitting was suggested over and over and over again. My first opportunity to apply the positivity training came a week later driving from Tennessee to my summer territory of Aiken, South Carolina as my Volkswagen Bug lost power. Dropped off in Hendersonville, NC Memorial weekend with no mechanic available until Monday, we slept in a foggy field and awoke the next day to mooing cows in this unbeknownst cow pasture. This was the first of dozens of car breakdowns for me and my team over the next five summers and gave me valuable life lessons. It taught me to go into problem-solving mode rather than emotional freak out mode. Little did I know then that problem-solving is made 100 times easier when emotions are calm because the brain thinks we are safe and does not activate stress hormones, which serve to tighten our muscles, quicken our breath, and increase our heartbeat to prepare us to run or hide for survival's sake.

I returned the following four summers to sell books door to door and recruit students in the spring following Paul's model—talk for 1.5 hours about the importance of self-confidence, learning to talk to people, work ethic, the value of positive thinking and then use the last 30 minutes to spring the job at hand... pay to attend a week of sales school in Nashville, Tennessee, relocate, find a place to live, and knock on doors selling Bible reference books for 12 hot summer weeks anywhere in the USA. Those summers severely exercised my mind's ability to stay positive, determined, and committed. Working 75 hours a week every summer, being responsible for the mental uplift of seven to 20 students I had recruited and being a positive role model for two to three roommates tested my mental capacities in ways I could have never imagined.

If pared down to the most significant lesson learned over five summers of 9000 in-home demos, 75-hour workweeks six days a week, endless days of 98 °F sweltering temperatures, 1000 door slams, 50 car problem incidents, countless flat tires, countless houses I erred in going into and had to get myself out of, two deaths, one near-death escape with an assault, responsibility for 60 recruited college student book sellers, assisting over 20 summer living arrangement searches for my team and myself across the south and Missouri, and 3000 pounds of book deliveries, the life lesson in two words would be tenacity and attitude. I learned self-hypnosis without realizing it. Every day was filled with self-affirmation and self-push. Some days I threw in the towel and found some woods, laid on a blanket, stared at the sky, and wondered what life was all about. Every time I hear Jose Feliciano's, "Listen to the Falling Rain," I am 19 years old in my Volkswagen Bug, as it's storming steamy summer rain, feeling happy to have a few moments of escape before getting back on track to resume my 30 demos for the day in sweltering Mississippi heat and face the prospect of rejection plus doors slammed in my face. Many days the attitude struggle was raging war. The factions were "You can do this" versus "I hate this and want to quit." Most days the "You can do this"' won but certainly not every single day. I had seven to twenty college students on my team each summer I was responsible for after persuading them to join the team and board the train headed to Attitude and Perseverance Ville. That kept those quitting attitudes from gaining too much traction. The dozens of problem-solving experiences encountered every day—going into houses I never should have, zero sales by 5:00 p.m., fighting the need for a nap, attitude sinking, aiding my roommates having attitude challenges, dealing with my team members wanting to quit and go home—constantly pushed my thoughts to say the right words, give the right encouragement, and help myself and others move into belief systems of "I can do this." In sales school, we had been trained to view *nothing as impossible*. This philosophy creates a bit of fearlessness, and I have the Southwestern Company to thank for suggesting this over and over again. When you think something enough, positive or negative, it becomes your truth. Like Henry Ford said, "Whether you think you can, or you think you can't—you're right." Hypnotherapy sessions with thousands of clients and their diverse challenges have proven, without doubt, that human beings are in possession of everything they need to make any change they desire. Thoughts are often stronger than steel, which is optimum when thoughts serve our purpose. When they serve as a detriment to happiness, peace, and productivity, the miracle of our brain is its capability to melt the steel into tired powerless shriveled up annoyance that, like a pesky fly, can be swatted away.

During this period of college and Southwestern sales and recruitment, my mother was recruiting on her own turf because soccer did not exist in Greensboro. She found the absence of organized youth soccer unacceptable after the family moved from Atlanta back to Greensboro. Stonewalled by the mayor and Parks and Recreation, Barbara Blum (Mom) pounded on doors, knocking with fervor, annoying the mayor, and refused to accept no. She organized 50 moms on a phone campaign to call the decision-makers who heard 50 mothers demand a youth soccer program. The return call finally came.

"Mrs. Blum, if you find the coaches, we will give you the fields."

She found coaches at Guilford College. Youth soccer was born. She opened a soccer shop and created a state organization structure so any town across NC would be supported in startup efforts. After arranging an international youth soccer tournament, Barbara had to beg Grimsley High School for fields. When Principal Glenn refused, her editorial ran in the newspaper, and he changed his tune.

I learned from my mother that if something doesn't exist, go out and make it happen. There were so many things I wanted for my children that didn't exist, so I developed them—a community children's chorus, a preschool program thriving 25 years later, creative writing and drama programs, tennis teams, campfire clubs, a children's yoga program. I don't share this to toot my horn but to encourage parents to develop what doesn't exist for your children.

A poem penned during that period expresses exhaustion, but it always passes. The results far outweigh a short period of being like a 20-year-old carpet... worn out!

I Want to be a Cow

- I want to be a cow and just moo
- Have nothing to do but a cud to chew
- Nowhere to go
- Just takin' it slow
- I want to be a cow and just moo

Years ago, a cardiologist from India, Dr. Matan Kataria developed a program for the sake of just laughing. He saw a difference in the physical healing of patients who watched funny movies during recovery. His program is called laughter yoga. People gather for no reason except to laugh, led by facilitators trained in very silly exercises. You can learn about it and see some of the exercises through Google. Laughter is another way to increase brain release of endorphins and serotonin, the brain chemicals producing a natural high from gut-wrenching laughter. Laughter builds bridges and breaks down walls. Before Covid I facilitated multiple laughter yoga groups. It's no surprise that this area pulled me in. The daughter of a bra and girdle salesman, you can imagine the humor and jokes we heard growing up. My dad was a humorist, a music lover, and verbally comical, always begging our dog Poochie to say three words so he'd never have to work again. Jack Blum (Dad) went out of his way to speak with everyone. His philosophical comments to the most mundane of topics delivered with humor and clever one-liners created an entertainment show before my eyes. From a young age, I observed how humor equalizes all exchanges and bonds complete strangers together. Humor in a family keeps stress and anxiety at bay.

When newly married, my mother-in-law visited us for the first time. I threw the shells from a cracked egg in the sink. I heard a gasp and a deeply serious voice.

"Lori! Look what you did!"

"What did I did?" I responded playfully to her shocked seriousness.

She picks up half the cracked eggshell out of the sink and scoops some remaining egg white out of the half shell. "Look how much egg you wasted." Her mouth was in a scowl. My mother-in-law grew up in the Great Depression. Her mother was a deaf mute. Her father died when she was three. She must have experienced extreme poverty.

"Oh, my god!" I said dramatically. Then I leaned way over and stuck my rear end into her stomach. "Spank me, Evelyn. I deserve it." Her laughter erupted; drama averted. Laughter distracts many situations away from volatility. Hail to laughter!

As a non-conformist it is no surprise my field is hypnosis, a modality supported by the American Medical Association since 1959, but a field that does not conform to the rational understanding for change. The change I help facilitate in partnership with my clients comes from a dreamy state in which our imagination is activated and tapped to overcome habits, blocks, and attitudes. I am not someone to hypnotize anyone, much less make them quack like a duck. I am someone who de-hypnotizes those who believe they *can't*. In partnership, we can change the quack like a duck to roar like a lion. Having worked with thousands of clients who seek change, it is a fact that the brain is capable of seismic change.

How were you able to transform a setback into a setup for success?

After marriage to my husband Barry and a move to Georgia, the state deemed my NC master's degree in school counseling and yearlong work experience insufficient for employment in Georgia schools without additional internships and two courses. Some walls we figure a way to climb around or through or over to stay the course. I rebelled at this wall and said forget it. The next 10 years my work included serving a philanthropist who needed help and persuasion giving away money and developing a senior activity offering 22 classes a week with transportation across metro Atlanta to our site.

One day in 2006, a wrong turn put me in front of Atlanta National Hypnosis Institute (ANHI). The sign intrigued me. Several experiences flashed across memory looking at that sign. One was the biofeedback experiment in college. The second experience was a living arrangement I agreed to at the Athens Mental Health Hospital in the mid '70s. I was provided a free room (without a lock). In return, I agreed to play the piano for residents two hours a day and share one meal a day. Diagnoses of the population included severe OCD, multiple personalities, developmentally delayed, and other conditions. Realizing how little I knew about the brain, I enrolled in ANHI that day for three years of study in the right-left brain science of ideas, beliefs, and change. Over the years, additional study has included Australian based HypnoFit for deep dive emotional release and study with integrative pediatrician Dr. Laurence Sugarman, on staff at Upstate Medical University in Rochester, NY. Children and teens are *amazing* to work with. It empowers them to feel they are in charge of change through their minds.

The study and practice of clinical hypnotherapy gives me expertise with tools to help others grow personally, emotionally, socially, professionally, artistically, athletically, assertively, courageously, forgivingly, and the growth is endless across all avenues I could not have implemented as a school counselor. Our brains are so capable of change, and much more so in the theta state of brain waves versus the conscious state that is full of "I can'ts" and defense mechanisms. My passion is showing you how to wake up the control you are capable of to make changes for a better life through the imaginative horsepower of your brain.

> *"Thinking is the hardest work there is, which is probably the reason why so few engage in it."*
> —Henry Ford.

Our conscious mind is the thinker. But the subconscious mind is the doer, without second guessing.

What unique formula, framework, or feature do you offer to your community or clients?

As the country pivoted to online everything, so did I. Zoom has proven viable and even preferred by many. During Covid I provided a 30-minute lunchtime hypnosis session for stress relief to the medical staff at the Decatur, Georgia VA. Clients began requesting Zoom, and today 70 percent of my clients experience hypnosis in the comfort of their homes through Zoom. As things continue to open, my high school program for Quit Vaping is gearing up for the fall. Vaping is a silent epidemic done without smell or detection in the bathroom and completely rampant.

I invite you to a complimentary consultation regarding areas of challenge you or family members of any age wish to resolve and/or any organizational needs or speaker presentation on the brain and hypnosis.

What information can be exchanged across multiple generations?

There are two dates on a gravestone, and we each have a tiny slice of 80–85 years to fill that dash. We are entitled to peace, happiness, and accomplishment in the dash of life. Dorothy had the capability to go home to Kansas the entire time in Oz but didn't know the ruby slippers held the power. Each one of us is in possession of ruby slippers called "imagination." Imagination is like a treadmill that is active early on but over time becomes stationary and collects dust. Imagination is present, alert, and tappable for more than nighttime dreaming. Our brains can shift, change, move forward, release, let go, and adapt. I've witnessed it a thousand times as a practitioner of clinical hypnosis. Feeling in control of our life is a pillar, a foundation of security. Even taking risks, which demands we allow control to float a bit out of our hands, is easier with a foundation of internal security of one's ability.

What do you want to be remembered for?
What is your ultimate legacy?

I hope I will be remembered as someone who cared deeply for the well-being of others. I hope to be remembered as a loving mother, wife, sister, and friend who had a great big laugh and a creative spirit. If I can help others make the dash of life happier, more fulfilling, more forgiving, and less stuck in the past, my dash will be a life well lived.

How can people connect with you?

I can be found at lorisugarman.com, pediatrichypnosis.com, and on instagram@lorisugarwriter.

THE LEGACY WE LEAVE IS NOT THE THINGS WE POSSESS BUT WHAT WE BRING OUT IN OTHERS.

by Tabatha Thorell

CHAPTER 20

CALLED TO BE ELITE
BY TABATHA THORELL

My body trembled as I sat hugging my knees on my bathroom floor. "Why can't I make this work?" I asked myself. "Why do I have this dream in my heart if I can't make it come true? It must just be me. I am the problem. I have spent so much time and money on courses, programs, coaches, masterminds, and seminars. Why can't I seem to make it work?" I cried out these horrible questions as tears fell down my cheeks. I just sat there and sobbed, waiting for an answer for what seemed like forever.

This wasn't the first time that I found myself in that position. It had been two years since I started my coaching business, and I struggled to make money consistently. I had been coaching people in one way or another for over a decade, but now I got a chance to do it my way, and I was struggling.

"What was I missing?" What wasn't I doing? What did I need, as a coach, to become wildly successful?" These questions haunted me because I thought I was doing all the right things. I studied and learned sales and marketing, paid for coaches and masterminds, implemented what I learned, and still struggled.

As I was asking myself these questions, new questions started to arise, "Do other coaches feel like this? Why do a majority of the coaches quit within 18 months of their business? Why are only a select few successful in the coaching world?"

After asking myself those questions, I realized that I wanted to help coaches, but not just in the traditional way. I wanted something fresh and new, incorporating everything you need as a coach to succeed. People always try to sell you the next best thing, or they market to you, telling you this one thing will make you millions. It's never one thing. A lot of little things are strung together to create a formula for success. After struggling for so many years (way beyond the two years on my own), I wanted to string together the things that make people successful and offer something to coaches that would help them at the highest level.

Where have you been called to lead?

I have been called to lead coaches, specifically moms who are coaches and want to create a wildly successful business. After realizing who I wanted to help, I had to figure out the best way I could serve them. I knew moms who were coaches needed something a little different. Trying to balance work and home life is a non-existent goal, especially when you work from home. There is no balance, just steps in the right direction towards peace, joy, success, and fulfillment. I am a mom to five beautiful daughters, and I run a coaching business from home so I can relate.

As a mom, you tend to put everyone before yourself. As a coach, you tend to do the same. That doesn't leave a lot left for you. If you don't take care of yourself, and if you don't have the right support system and the right resources, you can burn out quickly.

When I began coaching, I worked for other people and participated in building someone else's empire. I let fear get in the way of branching out sooner. I didn't know how I could raise my kids, help with my husband's businesses, be a good wife, and run a business. Have you ever let the excuses and unknowns block you from your destiny? I did for over ten years! I did not want that for other coaches.

I saw a lot of gaps in the marketplace, and I wanted to make things easier and more efficient for them. I had spent thousands of dollars on coaching programs and courses that filled me with a lot of empty promises, and I knew I wanted to be different. I also wanted to create a place where people feel valued, significant, connected, and certain they would get what they need to build a financially successful coaching business. I know with my experiences, I could help them save time, money, and heartache.

What unique formula, framework, or feature do you offer your community or clients?

I have spent much time and money on coaching programs and masterminds. Those experiences taught me a lot about what works and what doesn't. I have been burned by other coaches and taken advantage of by other businesses. Right before the Covid pandemic, I bought a high-ticket coaching program that offered me solutions to marketing. In my head, I was thinking, "If I could just solve my marketing problem, I would get my clients and finally become successful."

I researched this certain coach; he had many testimonies, and his sales team said all the right things. His marketing was spot on in attracting me as a client. I bought into his promises and was very hopeful for the outcome. Then came time for the reality of the program, which was incredibly disappointing. What he described in the sales funnel and on the sales call was not what was delivered. To top it all off, they made me feel like I was the problem. They glorified this coach and made me feel like a loser.

At first, I was angry at him. How could someone promise something and then not deliver, especially at a high-ticket price point! It was hard to understand how someone could be in the coaching space and hold no accountability to morals or ethics.

Then I became mad at myself. How could I be so stupid for falling for their marketing. I should know better about the strategies they use, and I fell right into them. My anger soon turned into self-doubt.

Maybe they are right. Maybe it is me? I can't seem to make anything work, and I don't even trust myself. What will my husband think? I am such a disappointment.

After self-doubt came fear, I became fearful of trying new things and trusting people, including myself. I started to pull back from reaching out for help. I stopped searching for the right coach, and most importantly, I stopped taking the risks I needed to take to grow my business. I felt defeated and hopeless, which is what brought me to that day on the bathroom floor.

Those thoughts were not serving me well, so after months and months of self-doubt and fear, I decided to look at things differently. I looked at the positive things that happened from that experience. I took a risk. I paid for a high-ticket program. I didn't let fear of money stop me from finding the solution I needed. Allowing myself to do that opened my mind to spend that kind of money on growth. I broke the scarcity mindset that had been plaguing me for years. This would serve me greatly in the near future.

I also wrote down everything I did not like about the program. I wanted to remember those things so I could do them differently for my future clients. It was painful going back and realizing all of the things I was disappointed in, but it allowed me to realize who I wanted to serve and how I could serve them at the highest level.

It also made me realize that I was paying for an external solution that I thought would solve all my problems. I needed a program that addressed my external problems like marketing and sales and internal issues like self-doubt and fear. I let self-doubt keep me stuck for months when I could have been moving forward in my business. I was focused on the tactics and strategies when I needed a coaching program that covered those areas and personal growth so that I could expand my business faster.

This experience may have caused some scars, but I developed a sense of sympathy for my clients with those scars. I understand what they need, and I am willing to give them that. I wanted to create a space where they get the tools they wanted and, more importantly, the identity they needed to transform their clients.

Elite: *"a select group that is superior in terms of ability or qualities to the rest of a group or society."*

My program, The Elite Coach Academy™ will transform you by allowing you to work internally on yourself and fill the gaps between becoming a coach and building a successful coaching business. It's one thing to want to be a coach and another to make it a successful business. I took principles from high-level masterminds, group coaching, done-for-you services, and done-with-you services and mashed them up for our unique system. This makes us unique and unlike any other coaching program out there. We have three main areas of focus:

Educating:

"If you are not growing, you are dying"
— Tony Robbins

We educate coaches with the tools they need to help them coach at the highest level and build a highly profitable coaching business. We want them to continue to grow as a coach and get true transformation for their clients.

Equipping:

We equip them with the skills and resources necessary to market and sell their services and when and who to hire in their business. We want them to have the best possible tools to become the top, elite coaches in the world while living the life they love.

Empower:

We empower women by creating an environment where they can thrive and take action on what they have learned. We create an environment of connection, collaboration, and action-oriented experiences.

What role does collaboration have in your current business?

If you look at any area of success, you see collaboration. In music, you see singers collaborating to reach more people. In movies, you see more than one production company in the credits because they know that different perspectives give the movie depth. Many authors work together to create something more spectacular like this book. The same goes for business. The most successful businesses have partnerships or collaborations to help them succeed.

When I started, I was afraid of collaborations because I didn't know my worth. I thought because I was a nobody that no one would want to collaborate with me, but that is just not true. Everybody has something to give, and everyone is valuable. When you collaborate, you take people's strengths and mash them together, creating a better experience for the audience and more credibility for the experts. Collaboration creates an acceleration, and I believe this so much that we incorporated it into our program.

How have you pivoted, shifted, or expanded your business in the last few years?

When I first began coaching, I started in the fitness space, but I soon realized that personal and business development are where my heart truly lies. Over the last decade and a half, I have learned many incredible things about people, business, and mindset. I believe that my experiences with money and the struggles I have faced in my own business have given me a unique perspective on helping others.

Have you ever had fear paralyze your ability to move forward in your business? I have. Have you ever had limiting beliefs about your worth or what you should charge someone for your services? I have. I can sympathize with those things because I have lived them and conquered them. This allows me to help others in a deeper, more impactful way.

What life or business lessons have created the most growth for you?

There are two lessons that I live by in my business and my personal life:

1. Time is incredibly more valuable than money.

   I come from a very hard-working family, and my parents taught me the value of hard work, morals, ethics, and loyalty. I am very grateful for this, but they didn't mention the value of time. They believed that if you can do it yourself, you should save the money you would have spent hiring someone. When I started my business, I knew this thinking hindered my growth. I tried to learn and implement everything myself, causing slow progression, confusion, and frustration. In The Elite Coach Academy™, we teach coaches when and how to hire the people that will help them accelerate quickly. Success loves speed, so when you can hire people to help you speed up your success, you will reach your goals faster and enjoy the process much more.

   You will also gain back more time with the ones you love or enjoy doing things you love. This is by far the best we could give you. You can always make more money but never get back more time.

2. Invest in yourself more than anything else, and it will pay dividends until the day you die.

   This lesson was taught to me early on in my journey. I learned that when you take the time to learn and grow, you have more to contribute to others. When you have more to contribute, you always have a way to earn money and create an impact. Even during moments of frustration and despair, I always took the time to learn and grow. Sometimes it was just listening to a podcast or an audio course. I knew if I did that, when those moments of despair passed, I would be a better person. I also changed my thinking on spending money on things that helped me grow. Even if it was for my personal growth. I also phrase it as investing rather than spending because with an investment, you always get a return. My return may come in the form of money, but it is not limited to that. It can also be the return of patience, love, joy, understanding, kindness, acceptance, the list goes on and on.

How were you able to transform a setback into a setup for success?

During my entrepreneurial journey, I have learned that a setback can be a setup for success if you have the right mindset. The day I sat on my bathroom floor and cried out for help was a moment I thought was a setback. I had tried something, yet again, and it didn't work. I felt helpless and was starting to feel hopeless.

"When the darkness surrounds us, the smallest light can show us the way out."

I wasn't gaining clients, and I couldn't understand why. I was in a dark place, but I kept hearing a quiet voice inside my head that said, "Ask the right questions." So I took a step back and asked, "If I had to make this work, what would I do? Who do I really want to serve? How can I help them at the highest level?"

These questions allowed me to develop a program that will significantly change people's lives if they allow it. If I had success in the other areas I was pursuing, I know I wouldn't have created The Elite Coaching Academy™. The setback became the setup.

What is the *why* behind what you do?

Helping others was always a desire I had in my heart, but my true *why* comes in two forms. First, my five daughters. They are all unique, beautiful, and impressionable. I want to impress upon them that you can make an impact and be an incredible, present mother as a woman. I show them that persistence, passion, positivity, and purpose can change the world, and your dreams were given to you for a reason. I want to give them more experiences, memories, and moments together as a family. Above all I want to be a great role model for them and make them proud.

Second, I have a deep calling to help other people thrive. If I can help in some way, then it is my privilege to be a part of that. I believe we all want to be good, create good, and do good things. One of my absolute favorite things is to see people energized and excited for life.

What do you want to be remembered for?
What legacy do you want to leave?

That's a very good question. I have often thought about this question over the years, but it hit me when my mom passed away in 2015. She battled an illness for over half her life, and with that came challenges she never saw coming. When you have someone you love battle something for so long, you become one of three things: You fight, letting passion lead the way. You freeze, letting empathy lead the way. Or you flee, letting avoidance lead the way. I fought.

I fought for my mom for as long as I can remember, even as a young child. The illness took a turn for the worse during the last five years of her life. I felt like she was giving up. This led me to become angry and view my mom in an unloving way. I saw all of her faults and chose to criticize her actions from my viewpoint. I am not proud of this, but this was my reality.

I chose to be a fighter for many years, but when it came time to say goodbye, I chose to freeze and let empathy lead the way. I told her I loved her and how proud I was to have her as my mom. I let go of all the anger and pride and loved her. I used my passion in a way that was freeing for her and me.

When it came time to speak at her funeral, I didn't think about how angry I was or the thoughts of criticism I had. I began thinking of all the things I loved about her and the ways she impacted my life. I remembered the great things she taught me and how I became

CALLED TO SPEAK, LEAD, AND IMPACT

the woman I am because of her. That's the thing about people who truly love you. They remember the good. My passion, persistence, and positivity are all things I am because of her.

The legacy we leave is not the things we possess but what we bring out in others. My mom brought out passion, persistence, and positivity because of what she went through. I learned, from her struggles, how to overcome obstacles and tragedies. That's what I hope to do for others: bring out their greatness by learning from my experiences. That is the legacy I want to leave.

How can people connect with you?

I can be found at tabathathorell.com and on Instagram @TabThorell.

THE AMAZING REALIZATION
THAT CAME WITH MY DECISION
TO LEAD IS THAT I DIDN'T
HAVE TO BECOME A DIFFERENT
PERSON, AN EXTROVERT,
A SUPERSTAR. I ONLY HAD
TO BECOME THE HIGHEST
ASPECT OF ME. IT WAS ALL
ABOUT WHO I WANTED AND
NEEDED TO BE AND
WHO I ALLOWED MYSELF
TO SHOW UP AS.

by Arianne Traverso

CHAPTER 21

BE, CREATE, INSPIRE: THE SUCCESS FORMULA BY ARIANNE TRAVERSO

Lima, Peru circa 1987. It's 8:00 p.m., and my parents are driving through the empty streets of Lima with a white flag on their car because they need to get me to my doctor as I had a fever of 104 degrees for over a day, only to get the bad news that the antibiotic I needed to save my life was not available in any pharmacy, and we had to resort to the black market.

This was actually normal for us from 1985–1989 when the country was in a state of terror and economic instability.

The terrorist group Shining Path had descended into the capital and car bombs would explode in the city center. News of kidnaps and assassinations filled the conversations of people trying to live their fear-ridden daily lives.

You see, I am one in a million. An autoimmune, genetic condition called cyclic neutropenia was passed down from my mom and made me prone to infections that for normal people are insignificant, but for me are life-threatening.

What happened in the next 12 months would ultimately change my fate and what is now the life I lead. We fled my native country of Peru in 1989 to escape fear, violence, lack of access to food and most importantly, medicine and to ultimately give my brother and me the

American dream and a chance to a life with freedom and safety. I like to call this the beginning of my future and possibilities.

Even though I can't eliminate the autoimmune condition, it's actually shaped who I am. It would've been really easy for me to fall back in school, miss a ton of extra days because I was sick, and feel less than the other kids. I would get massive cold sores all over my mouth and lips that were pretty gross to a nine-year-old or such severe sore throats that I couldn't eat or talk. But I went to school with two Tylenol pills in my backpack and a thermometer in case of a fever. My mom would tell me if I had a fever to ask to go to the restroom and take my Tylenol and go back to class. I was so good at not letting my illness get in the way of my social life, my sports, and grades.

This meant I was always top of my class, getting honors and awards for academic excellence, and always being among the popular kids. I used my illness as a source of strength and made it a nothing to worry about thing by brushing it aside.

When I look back at the now 40 years of living this way, I see why I have the resilience and the determination to live a life I love and appreciate and why entrepreneurship was almost my only option to be totally happy and free.

Many use a word to describe this feeling of being in charge of your life, of living your dreams and crafting your ideal way of moving through the world, your calling. I actually didn't discover my calling. I didn't find it. It was always there as a non-negotiable! Nothing in me ever wanted to be an employee working for someone. I look back now, and I think it was because subconsciously I didn't want to be constrained by my illness. I thought about the uneasy conversations I'd potentially have to have. But more than that, being my own boss gave me a sense of accomplishment and purpose that filled my independent, I can do anything, overachiever pocket.

Let me also add something here. Apart from being a super A+ student, I was also a rebel and a self-proclaimed bohemian. It was these two polarities that created a recipe for a creative non-conformist and a perfect candidate for entrepreneurship and teaching others that they too can lead the life they love and desire!

Being your own boss is not for the faint of heart. You need to have certain qualities:

- Strength
- Determination
- Audacity
- Grit
- Flexibility
- Kindness
- Passion
- Fervor

It's not often that a company starts and lasts for more than five years. Actually, 45 percent of businesses don't make it to five years (Bureau of Labor Statistics). This is why I became a business coach for people wanting to start their own passion-based business. Because doing something you love shouldn't mean putting it on the back burner because you lack the how-tos for it. I've started several businesses since I was in university, and they all progressively became a little bigger and more complicated.

My first business was designing customized sports posters for kid athletes. I then opened a small graphic design firm. I got bit by the yoga bug and became a full-time yoga teacher (which FYI you're an entrepreneur because pretty much no one hires you as an employee), but I digress. I really owned being a yoga-preneur as I taught teacher trainings, retreats and workshops worldwide, which then allowed me to open a yoga studio, then purchase a yoga trade show, and ultimately become an entrepreneurship coach. There was something I felt when I taught my first class that I had never felt before, and it took me a while to understand. It was being a leader! This was the missing link to my transition from being a freelancer to a business owner. This was the awakening inside of me that helped me feel confident and committed to seeing my life unfold on my own terms.

Where have you been called to lead?
What is the *why* behind what you do?

This essence of leadership began permeating all aspects of my life which started to blossom. I am naturally a huge introvert and being in front of people was actually quite difficult, but it wasn't until I was invited to teach at the German Yoga Conference that I knew I had a new destiny mentoring others and helping them find their spark. There was a deep-rooted desire to see others empowered, able, and ready to express themselves in a new way with a voice and presence.

This was the shift when I considered myself an adult and when I also considered myself a business owner as opposed to a freelancer. And what I understood and felt deep inside was that when creating a business, you need the following:

1. A vision you truly believe in
2. A monetary goal that is hairy and scary
3. A map to help you get there
4. A guide to help you get there faster

Many people don't think #4 is essential, but I assure you, building a business alone will make the road longer and less supported. I can close my eyes and see the people who made me a better teacher, a better mother, a better business owner, and who helped me overcome some pitfalls.

I remember my teacher telling me that I only had to be connected to the larger aspect of the transformation I was providing others and to let divine wisdom lead the way. I understood what surrendering to my confidence, my strength, and my resilience really felt like. And here's the most important piece. As a mentor and guide, it's not about me; it's all about the shifts I can help others make!

The amazing realization that came with my decision to lead is that I didn't have to become a different person, an extrovert, a superstar. I only had to become the highest aspect of me. It was all about who I wanted and needed to be and who I allowed myself to show up as.

When I started seeing the transformation in my students and clients, it gave me such a rush of fulfillment and happiness. This is what helped me transition from teaching to leading to coaching.

What unique formula, framework, or feature do you offer to your community or clients?

Now as a business and marketing coach, I focus on a different kind of transformation and having a system to help an idea go from thought to creation is extremely valuable. Because I am a holistic coach, I make sure to bring the aspects of life and business together to create a seamless design.

This framework is a combination of two parts: the AAAA blueprint and the FLOW system. We'll start with the four As as they summarize the journey, which is the backbone of my BFA Program, (business freedom accelerator).

- **Assess:** The law of tensegrity states that for you to plan where you want to go, you need to understand where you are. Assessing your current business and life helps you create a strategic vision plan to where you want to go in a way that doesn't make it feel impossible or extremely far away.

- **Align:** This is a magical word that fits into so many aspects of business and life. Here we focus on your strengths and abilities to create the precise way you want to work and lead your life and business. It's how you recognize your innate superhero qualities to set a business model, a marketing strategy, and a delivery of your goods or services.

- **Activation:** There's no change in anything unless you put things into action. Activating yourself to *do* your daily tasks and projects is the *only* way you'll get to where you want to go. Consider this the movement part of your business, whereas the two points above are the more meditative aspects.

- **Accountability:** I know you have a fire in you that wants to help you move forward. We all do to some degree. Here's the best part of this, though. When you have someone holding you accountable, you get to where you want to go faster. And I don't know about you, but I want to get there faster and with ease. Finding someone to keep you accountable is the most effective way to keep your goals in check.

Understanding the four As blueprint helps set you up to create a **FLOW** strategy to seeing your goals, projects, and actions set into place.

- **Fun for Freedom:** Any big endeavor has many moving pieces to it, many parts that can seem daunting. When you step into doing things with fun so that the end result is feeling free, then any task whether big or small will carry a different energy. Does implementing a marketing strategy seem like a nightmare to you, or can you switch your perspective and find the fun in it?
- **Leadership:** Being in charge of your success is a responsibility you want to feel proud of.

  I know when I stepped into being a leader and owning the qualities of a leader, it made everything I did and didn't do so much more powerful. Being responsible is the best quality you want to embody and then of course having a plan you can follow will help get you there quicker.
- **Omnipresence:** The word omnipresence is your go-to when you are looking at the more strategic part of creating the business results you desire. Especially for personal brands who want to grow, having a presence in your visibility is key. This mainly relates to marketing and networking, and I have a system that helps your visibility increase.
- **Willingness to Work:** As a coach and consultant I know that being willing to put in elbow grease is what gets results. When you're in the beginning stages of your business, you wear many hats, and as your business expands, more things come onto your plate. You have to be willing to do the work or delegate a team to get you there with more ease and grace.

Once you see these pillars as a framework, then the rest is fundamental strategies and tactics that fall into the core business model. Consider this, when putting together your ideal life, the way you generate funds to fuel that life, especially as an entrepreneur, is a combination of your daily actions, but without knowing what those are, you're basically walking blindly.

Ninety percent of your time should be focused on marketing and sales and more specifically, visibility, lead generation, conversions, and sales. Once I started implementing this rule, my business grew quicker. I got rid of excess tasks, created better boundaries and explored more efficient and effective ways of getting things done. When you decide to become fully invested in your organization and follow a plan, the results are attained quicker. Now don't get me wrong, sometimes you get derailed. A wrench gets thrown into the gears. Being resilient and so focused on your dreams and goals is what gets you back on track and ready to take ownership.

What information can be exchanged across multiple generations?

As a mother this is even more important as I want to raise my daughter with the same fervor and tenacity I have to create a world that inspires others. As a fourth-generation entrepreneur I know how important paving the road for my daughter is, to give her the strength to be a leader in her life, and to help others experience love, happiness, and greatness. Being willing to do the work is the key to unlocking your hidden potential. Resolving generational traumas, seeing the patterns and being open to changing them is what will help your legacy live on. And the best thing about this is that once you start the healing process, it helps resolve energetic binds that may have prevented your forward momentum.

Just as I mentioned previously, using the four As gives you an opportunity to create your own blueprint for your life, for what you want to leave the world and use the success you create to leave a footprint of hope and motivation for those who hear and see you.

Forward momentum isn't always possible because as you know, sometimes taking a few steps back will help you take many steps forward. Here's a motto I live by: See mistakes as opportunities to learn as opposed to seeing them as downfalls that keep you stuck. As a multiple business owner I've experienced many setbacks that sometimes made me feel like the world was falling apart and I wasn't cut out to be an entrepreneur. And you know what? Every time I implemented the strategy as a teacher, it made me stronger and helped me avoid that same mistake.

What role does collaboration have in your current business?

One of the most important pieces of this is the accountability—the fourth A. This is the perfect strategy for two different aspects: making sure what you said you wanted to do gets done and an opportunity to collaborate. Collaborating is one of the best strategies out there to market, grow your visibility, or get a project done. I'm not a big fan of partnerships but working together on a project can bring lots of synergy and bigger results. For example, I have a great relationship with a coach who certifies other coaches, and she brings me in to lead marketing trainings for her cohorts, which gets me great visibility, and usually I walk away with a few clients who are ready to start and grow their businesses. And on the same front, I promote her coaching certification to my community. It's a high level of cooperation and collaboration to get to your goals faster. I rely on the rule of everyone winning in this process, so make sure when you collaborate that there's clarity on roles, on actions, and expectations.

Not only that, but when you're doing visibility marketing and you collaborate with others with a complementary audience to yours, you're also showing up as a leader, as an expert which can help you in the client acquisition process. Marketing and growing my business with joint ventures is one of my favorite ways to invest my time and energy.

My ultimate goal with all these strategies, tactics, experiences, projects, and visions is to feel successful in everything I've accomplished and leave a positive imprint and legacy, first, for my daughter, and second, for other women who crave freedom and are ready to help others and keep the ripple effect moving. This is directly reflected on who I have to be for this to happen. What qualities do I want to embody and see the lessons that have created the most growth for me?

What life or business lessons have created the most growth for you?

Since I am obsessed with learning and experiencing the world, I'd say what has shaped me has been my fearless leaps into the unknown. I've traveled the world many times, seeing the most amazing places that are filled with rich history and inspiration. From meditating in the cave where a Hindu saint lived in solitude thousands of years ago, to hiking the Colca Canyon, the deepest in the world, to lecturing 500 women, these experiences have marked my desire to live to the fullest! I've hired the mentors who shaped my mindset from limited to possible and been in rooms with eight figure business owners because I know the people you surround yourself with will shape your habits and actions.

Because knowledge is power, I also make sure to listen to two to three audio books a month, invest in training to uplevel my skill sets, and dedicate time to being autodidactic. My grandfather was a self-made millionaire in Peru with only a sixth-grade education and from an immigrant family, so I know anything is possible if you set your mind to it.

What do you want to be remembered for?
What is your ultimate legacy?

What's important here is basically understanding you are the designer of your life. You are in charge of being the person you admire, of creating the outcomes you dream of and inspiring others through that process. Leaving a legacy of correct action, selfless contribution, respect, truth, and love is why I do what I do. It's my duty to make sure I leave things better than how I found them in society and in my home. I believe that my daily contributions to inspire other women are the foundation of a better personal economy which helps the web of our society stay connected. I'd like to be remembered as a positive influence who gives back to the community as a mentor and teacher as well as a physical imprint by donating to organizations that support educating others who are less fortunate, and for saving our planet. A consistent mantra that I rely on is from the Native American Indian-Iroquois Law: "In our every deliberation, we must consider the impact of our decisions on the next seven generations."

I have one ask of you at this moment. Take a pause and a big deep breath, allow your biggest dreams and goals to fill every cell of your body, visualize who you want to be, what you want in life, and commit to taking daily steps, whether small or large to get where you want to go. Experience the journey fully with love, conviction, and confidence.

How can people connect with you?

I can be found at bizyogi.co and on Instagram @ari.biz.yogi.

WHEN WE LEAD WITH OUR
HEART AND LEAD WITH LOVE,
WE MAKE OURSELVES
HAPPIER AND THAT SPILLS
OUT TO EVERYONE
AROUND US.

by Marcia Narine Weldon

CHAPTER 22

I WROTE A EULOGY FOR THE MAN WHO TRIED TO KILL ME BY MARCIA NARINE WELDON

For a long time, every time I saw someone with the shape of his head or the cut of his shoulders, I would stop frozen in my tracks, even though I knew he lived in another state. Even if I hadn't seen him in years, he still had the power to paralyze me, if only for a moment, even in his absence. Years before, he almost did paralyze me. More importantly, he almost killed me more than once.

One time, he threw me against the wall with our newborn in my arms, causing me to see stars and be dizzy for weeks. Another time, he punched through my car windshield, stopping less than half an inch from my eye. I watched his fist barrel towards my face at warp speed while shards of glass rained on me in what seemed like slow motion. When I gingerly pulled tiny pieces of glass off of my lips and face, I said quietly, "You could have killed me and blinded the baby with glass." He laughed and said, "I know, and I want you to know that too. I can kill you whenever I want to." For years, including my entire pregnancy and even after we broke up, I slept with a knife under the bed.

Over the years we spent together, I called the police repeatedly, but that was never a deterrent. On one occasion, half a dozen New York City police officers came to my home, and he told them to shoot him out— otherwise known as suicide by cop. The next day, I packed up my son and moved back to Miami where I grew up. I left all of my furniture behind, but I had most of my clothes packed already. I knew the day would come when I would have to flee.

But months later, I allowed him back into my life. Optimistically, foolishly, and maybe due to post-pregnancy hormones, I thought that he would want to be a better person for his baby, even though I never left my son alone with him. Our reconciliation was short-lived. People often asked why I didn't get a restraining order, but I knew that filing could mean signing my own death warrant. He actually started to choke one of his girlfriends in a public parking lot because she was taking my side on an issue, although we had never met. When I learned about another woman he was hurting, I paid for her and her children to move out of the state. Every building I worked or lived in had his picture at the front desk so security could alert me if he showed up.

Because of him, I lived in my own personal hell for more than half of my life. But he was my son's father, and I had a lifelong connection to him. He was also one of the most intelligent, generous, kind, charismatic, loving, funny people you could ever meet until he drank. Sober, he lit up every room that he entered. He also suffered from bipolar disorder, and the highs and lows could be sudden and fierce. Even so, on more than one occasion, I personally saw someone offer him a job that he hadn't applied for just because of his charm and engaging conversation. I have never met anyone like him, and I never will. My son is the special person that he is because of his father.

But as those who met him would learn, he could go from engaging to enraged at a moment's notice. Even after we no longer had contact, the connection from his heart to mine through our son almost killed me. Although it looked like I had everything together on the outside as a successful, high-paid corporate lawyer, on the inside I was in a constant state of simmering anger, resentment, and terror. If I saw a certain look in an actor's eyes when he was threatening a woman on a movie screen, I felt like I was in imminent danger. I couldn't listen to certain songs on the radio without plunging into fear.

After I ended that relationship, I volunteered to represent women and children who had been beaten by people who loved them in court, even while I beat myself up for allowing myself to be a victim. The families that I helped had limited choices and means. What was my excuse? Why was I still a prisoner of this person who was no longer calling or threatening me? Why did I freeze if someone called from his area code? I had graduated from Harvard Law School and had the wherewithal and support to do better. I had great therapists. What was wrong with me?

Over the years, my experience with my son's father caused two seemingly irreconcilable reactions. I became hard-hearted and cold. I didn't trust anyone to get close to me. I had experienced abuse from a family friend as a child, and those memories would come flooding back seemingly at random. But of course, there was a connection. So I grew an impenetrable protective shell around my heart so that no one could enter, not friends, not lovers, and not co-workers. At the same time, I also opened my heart and poured into strangers who needed help because that was safe for me. I felt good that I could help them with their pain, even as I stuffed mine down in my body. My heart was always full of love to give to others. My heart was also, ironically, so empty.

Then I fell in love with a wonderful man. My heart accidentally opened up to a non-stranger. He accepted me with my flaws and fears. He accepted my son with the mental illness that he had inherited from his father. He soothed me when I had nightmares or panic attacks when I thought about my ex. He said he would never leave when my son had a mental health crisis right after our wedding. When my son's paternal grandfather died, he flew with me to the family home to pay my respects and to protect me in case my ex stepped out of line. My ex's mother even came to my wedding. It was perfect until it wasn't. A few years after we got married, he filed for divorce right at the start of the Covid pandemic. The pressure of dealing with my son and his hospitalizations for mental illness was too much for him and our marriage to bear.

I didn't realize it, but all of this collective trauma was slowly and silently killing me. My blood pressure was often off the charts no matter what I ate, how much I exercised, or how many times I saw my therapist. My doctors told me I needed to work less and relieve the stress of being a lawyer and business owner. But I knew that wasn't the case. I was a unicorn among my friends—an ecstatically happy lawyer who loved work and thrived in it even when no one else I knew in my profession did. Through the worst of the abuse from my son's father, I never missed work or even a deadline because of it. But somehow, years after leaving my ex, dealing with personal issues landed me in the hospital six times in six years because of what doctors thought were heart attacks and strokes.

Losing my marriage, trying to keep my son from going into yet another mental hospital during Covid, and being isolated from everyone led to what I *thought* was my aha moment. Like many people during the pandemic, I tried to go inward to make sense of a senseless world where everything I knew and loved was dying. I became more serious about meditation and mindfulness. I started practicing reiki. I learned about tapping, otherwise known as emotional freedom technique (EFT). I went to a hypnotherapist and then learned it myself. I became a master neurolinguistic programming practitioner so that I could reprogram my mind. To distract myself from the pain, I went on to get certifications and specialized training in several more energy healing modalities. But even after all of that, I was still going to the hospital for heart attack scares and joking with my doctors that I might as well eat Cheetos and drink beer all day for all the good that the healthy, zen lifestyle had done for me.

Nothing changed until I had a conversation with one of my spiritual advisors, who told me that my heart would continue to attack me until I learned forgiveness. That was a no go for me. I knew that the issues with my heart were not physical. The hardness in my heart was because of the justifiable anger and rage I had towards the people who hurt me and let me down when I hadn't done anything wrong.

Sixty-two percent of American adults say they need more forgiveness in their personal lives, according to a survey by the nonprofit, Fetzer Institute. I was just not one of them. I was a lawyer who understood and sometimes reveled in scorched earth strategies to get justice for clients. In my mind, there was a clear right and wrong. If you were wrong, you needed to admit it, atone publicly, suffer, and make sure it never happened again.

But I also knew it was no coincidence that the issues that landed me in the hospital related to my heart, where the anger was, and my head, where I was constantly ruminating and reliving painful memories. My feelings and thoughts were literally killing me. I needed to save my life because I was too cute and too young to end up in the stroke ward again.

Here's what I learned about anger and forgiveness. Your brain scan actually looks different when you're angry, sad, or happy. Your emotions can tangibly affect your brain. Anger and hostility are linked to a higher risk of heart disease, and poorer health for people with existing heart disease. Chronic anger puts you into a chronic fight-or-flight mode, which floods your system with cortisol and results in changes in heart rate and blood pressure. This can lead to an increased risk of depression, heart disease, and diabetes. Forgiveness can actually calm stress levels, which can improve health. Scientists have found that among a subset of volunteers in an experiment who scored high on measures of forgiveness, high lifetime stress didn't predict poor mental health. It just zeroed it out. Studies from Johns Hopkins have found that the act of forgiveness can reduce stress, lower blood pressure, heart attack risk, and cholesterol, improve sleep, and reduce pain and anxiety levels.

So many of us are angry at people, and we don't even remember why. We don't remember who was wrong, but we are waiting for that apology before we move on with that person. Sometimes we wait for that apology, which may never come, before we can move on with our own lives. The anger, sadness, and resentment gets trapped in our bodies and makes us physically, mentally, and emotionally sick.

That's what had happened to me. I was angry at my son's father for causing me to live in a constant state of hypervigilance. I was angry at my husband for filing for divorce in the midst of my son's mental health crisis and my father's worsening dementia. I was angry at my son because I went through more than one retirement fund to pay for his rehab and other bills. I was angry at my family friend for abusing me as a child and then denying it when I finally had the courage to confront him.

I blamed them all for their poor character. I shamed them for their lack of discipline and integrity. I complained to everyone who would listen. I dwelled in the suffering. And I got sicker and sicker. So I knew something had to change. I wasn't going to get an apology, my retirement fund back, or a do-over of my childhood or marriage. Being angry and smug was eating away at my insides like battery acid.

Based on these studies and my own personal experience, the why was obvious. But how do you actually forgive someone who doesn't deserve it? First, it's important to differentiate between what forgiveness is and is not. It's not justice, reconciliation, weakness, letting someone get away with it, a call for reconciliation, or even a reward or byproduct of an apology. According to Bob Enright, who has studied forgiveness for over thirty years, it's about offering the person that hurt you something positive, whether it's empathy, compassion, or even understanding. That made sense to me because as I dove into more metaphysical pursuits and the study of Eastern philosophies, I started to see myself as one with everyone. I began to understand the benefits of detaching from the outcome and living in the present moment. And I started thinking about how much pain someone has to be in to hurt someone else to make themselves feel better. That made the process of forgiveness a bit easier, but it was still not easy, so I focused on learning about forgiveness like it was a full-time job.

Eventually, I started to lead with an open heart and with unconditional love no matter what. Scientists have actually discovered that there's an electromagnetic field that goes around the heart and can spread 8–10 feet. This is called the toroidal field, and you've already experienced it. Have you ever met someone, even a stranger, and just felt a beautiful energy from them? That's their aura and that comes from them having an open heart. When we lead with our heart and lead with love, we make ourselves happier and that spills out to everyone around us. The love from our heart is contagious, and we can light up a room just with our presence. In the same way, you can actually feel when someone has a closed heart, like I used to have.

This isn't just woo woo kumbaya stuff. When we are angry or frustrated, it affects our immune system. Just five minutes of upset can suppress the immune system for up to six hours. The good news is that having an open heart full of love and gratitude can strengthen your immune system. I used to get sick all the time. I joked that if someone sneezed a mile away, I would get sick. But when I started focusing on forgiveness, happiness, gratitude, and joy, my health actually improved.

I focused on two key things to strengthen my heart and my happiness level. First, I focused on self-love. That's easier said than done. But I spoke to myself the way I would speak to someone I love. I looked at myself in the mirror daily and I told myself affirmations that were specific to me. I never passed a mirror without saying silently or out loud, "I love you, gorgeous," with a smile. At first, I didn't believe the words, but I never stopped, not even to this day. Using my NLP training, I recorded my own voice with affirmations and fell asleep to it at night because in a state of sleep, my conscious mind couldn't try to talk me out of what I was saying. I focused on forgiving myself as the ultimate act of self-love. I stopped beating myself up and blaming, shaming, and complaining about my own circumstances. After I focused like a laser on loving and forgiving myself, I was ready to forgive others, not for them but for me.

I started using the Hawaiian forgiveness practice of ho'oponopono every day. Every day I picked a different person and put them before my mind's eye and said the following:

I love you.
I'm sorry.
Please forgive me.
Thank you.

Many days, I said this to myself while looking in the mirror. Some days I said it 108 times to no one in particular. I just repeated the phrases. Other days I imagined people who I thought had wronged me. Part of the exercise required me to ask them for forgiveness. So I did that through the prayer. I visualized speaking with people who would not be receptive to a difficult conversation, and then I did it in person when I could. Every morning during my prayer and meditation, I visualized hugging or gazing at the people who had wronged me with love and compassion. I envisioned them sending love and compassion back to my heart. I forgave people from generations back. I forgave people who committed heinous acts that I saw on the news. I watched and rewatched videos of people who have forgiven Nazis for the Holocaust, those who had committed genocide in Rwanda, and of mothers of murdered children.

I forgave my son's father even though every time he apologized, he would call me back minutes later in a rage. I forgave my ex-husband even though he didn't ask for it, but first I asked for forgiveness for the crazy life he had been thrust into right after we got married. I forgave the family friend who abused me, even as he denied it to himself and to me.

Now, I forgive very easily. It doesn't mean that I forget, but it's an automatic reflex because I've trained myself to forgive no matter what. Here's how I know that it works. First, almost nothing bothers me for long, not even traffic or politics. During the 2020 election, I went through my days with ease and grace as others, devastated by the pandemic and politics, grew more and more depressed and demotivated. When my ex-husband contracted COVID, I dropped food off at his house. When I got into a relationship with another person who suddenly scared me so much that I had to get a gun to protect myself, I forgave him and myself within 48 hours. I knew that

I would never remain in an abusive relationship again, but I could love him from a distance. I trained my heart to be permanently and unconditionally open.

In March 2022, my son's father died from alcohol poisoning. For years, I had secretly prayed for his death so that I could finally have some peace and a solid night's sleep, but I had long forgiven him before he died. When I learned about his death, I flew to his family home. I helped pick and edit pictures for the memorial program. As I looked at hundreds of pictures of him, I said the ho'oponopono prayer over them and prayed that he had found peace. I wrote a testimony to him for the program for his memorial, and I did it in love. I focused on the good that he had brought to my life. I even felt sadness like I had lost an old, troubled friend. I asked for some of his ashes to spread in a healing farewell ceremony.

I still explode now and then when I get angry. I don't want anyone to think that my new zen means that I float on a lotus flower chanting all day. But I am quick to seek forgiveness for an outburst. And when someone lashes out at me, I forgive them in my mind before and whether or not they ask for it. This forgiveness practice is not toxic positivity; rather, it's a way to get rid of the toxic anger that will lead you to a premature death. So try it.

I love you.
I'm sorry.
Please forgive me.
Thank you.

You'll feel lighter. Your heart will be open, and your love will radiate to others who really need it. Make sure to let love rule. Everyone has someone in their life they refuse to forgive or are seeking forgiveness and aren't getting it. The effects are beyond mental and psychological. Anger and resentment can kill you like it almost killed me. So here's my forgiveness formula:

- Forget what you think forgiveness is supposed to be
- Own your role, if any, and own your feelings. Think about whether you need to apologize before you forgive

- Resist the need to be right or get an apology
- Go at your own pace. Forgiveness takes time. Don't give up and don't worry about setbacks in the journey
- Investigate nontraditional tools to learn forgiveness
- Vanquish the victim mentality
- Enjoy the release and ease that comes from letting it go

Where have you been called to lead? What is the *why* behind what you do?

I specialize in coaching lawyers, compliance personnel, executives, entrepreneurs, and other high achievers who feel that they can't make mistakes or be vulnerable and who must always be and feel right. Once I started to publicly open up about my personal struggles with these issues, others reached out to me for guidance and advice on how they could change their own lives. I want to make it safe for professionals to fail, admit mistakes, ask for help, and lead from a place of vulnerability. For me, almost everything starts with forgiveness and unconditional love. So many of my clients are stuck and unhappy because they feel that they don't deserve their success—the classic imposter syndrome issue. A lot of that comes from conditioning or relationships they experienced in childhood or as young adults. They grow to hate themselves, their family members, and others, and they don't realize how that impacts them professionally today. They also learn that it's not safe to trust. This makes it difficult for them to practice trust-based leadership, which derails their effectiveness.

What unique formula, framework, or feature do you offer to your community or clients?

I take a holistic, neuroscience-informed, evidence-based approach looking at brain health, biological and psychospiritual factors, and social engagement to empower clients to make meaningful and sustained changes in their personal and professional lives. I call myself the lawyer/lightworker.

What life or business lessons have created the most growth for you?

My coaching business increased exponentially when I started to share personal information on social media, particularly the career-oriented LinkedIn. I thought I needed to stick to legal issues or science-based posts given what I thought my audience wanted and expected, but I got the most traction from sharing personal stories and lessons learned. The more vulnerable I was, the more public and private comments I would receive. That taught me the importance of being authentic and open. It was a risk worth taking. When you're open about what you've overcome, it's easier for people to know, like, and trust you.

What do you want to be remembered for? What is your ultimate legacy?

My most important contribution is to help people forgive the people who don't deserve it so that they can break the generational trauma that has held them and their families back. By working with one person at a time, I want to help one million people go from overwhelmed to overjoyed, from stressed out to serene, and from confused to clear on their personal and professional goals. Each person I touch can and should pass on what they've learned to someone else. I also want to be known for empowering people to do what they love and love what they do.

How can people connect with you (website and socials)?

I can be found at illuminatingwisdom.com and @IlluminatingWisdom on Instagram.

WHAT'S NEXT ON YOUR HORIZON?

The end of this book is the beginning of your journey to speak, lead, and impact.

There comes a time when you need to share your story, voice, and message, and you must speak it out loud because the desire in your heart is even bigger than your gut-wrenching fear.

This happened for me a decade ago when I left my corporate career and started speaking. I was terrified, excited, nervous, and elated all at the same time. Basically, I had no choice. It was clearly a predestined calling and therefore there was no turning back.

The speaking and coaching world was brand new to me. I began to search for a community of heart-centered entrepreneurs like yourself on a mission to serve humanity that would be inclusive, supportive, provide education, and be inspiring.

I looked high and low but couldn't find one, so I created a group and named it "The Speakers and Coaches Networking Society." I wrote out our vision, three core values, and one philosophy.

- To serve humanity at the highest level.
- The three Cs: community, connection, collaboration
- Philosophy: We vs Me
- Ten years later our group is thriving with 20,000 extraordinary members from all around the world.

During the pandemic our group served as a hub and home base for virtual conferences, meetups, and training that included speakers and attendees from almost every continent and country. We came full circle knowing we are better, stronger, and wiser together. Lastly, we are not alone.

Over the years we have built out an extensive library, and we offer a plethora of free resources, including a customized speaker's one sheet template for those who want to get booked for speaking opportunities such as keynotes, panels, and conferences.

Download yours at https://bit.ly/SpeakersOneSheetTemplate

Here are additional SAC Society resources available to you:

- Monthly meetings called "The Collective" where members come together online to connect and build strategic relationships with one another
- A complimentary listing in our speakers and coaches directory: https://speakersandcoaches.com/directory
- Monthly masterclasses and trainings on community building, professional speaking, and sales to grow your coaching business
- Ongoing five-day challenges held monthly with an emphasis on getting booked on stages and social media visibility http://www.SpeakersandCoaches.com

The founder, Wendi loves connecting with her readers on social media. Subscribe to her feed on IG and LinkedIn @wendiblumweiss and be sure to tag her with a photo holding this book. She will repost many of them. And remember…

It doesn't matter your age, income, or background, someone needs to hear your message, and that's why we created this community designed to nurture and support your growth as a speaker and coach.

Wendi Blum Weiss

ABOUT THE AUTHORS

WENDI BLUM WEISS

Wendi Blum Weiss is a former pharmaceutical account manager who changed professions at the age of 50 to become an impact driven business consultant, international speaker, author, and leadership coach. She is the founder of The Speakers and Coaches Networking Society, an organization that helps speakers, coaches, leaders, and entrepreneurs impact more lives through speaking, writing, and sharing their stories on multiple platforms to bring more positivity into the world.

She is considered one of the top experts in the field of personal mastery and professional leadership and has worked with individuals, organizations and companies from around the world to unleash their genius power.

Equally as important is her ongoing commitment to humanitarian endeavors as the central core philosophy of her life's work.

PATRICIA WOOSTER

Patricia is a former software executive turned founder of WoosterMedia Publishing, where they help experts, leaders, executives, and entrepreneurs convert their intellectual property into print and digital products so they can build brand awareness and reach a global audience. Her clients include C-Level executives, college professors, professional athletes, and media personalities. They have landed agents, major publishing contracts, speaking opportunities, and bestseller status.

She is the author of 16 books, including the awarding-winning and bestselling book *Ignite Your Spark* with Simon & Schuster and her bestseller *The Write Plan: How to Successfully Write & Publish a High-Impact Book.*

Patricia helps her clients amplify their message and leverage their expertise into books, digital courses, workshops, speeches, consulting, and media opportunities. Her experience ranges from working with companies and organizations like Disney, Home Shopping Network, WeDay, Informix Software, and KPMG to working with startup entrepreneurs and influencers.

Today, Patricia is the CIO of Designing Genius, a powerful training and SaaS platform that changes the paradigm of how companies and people reach their highest and greatest potential. She directs the in-house development of Designing Genius products and services while assisting clients and companies in the development of their brands through the use of our products, services, and tools.

LEAVE A REVIEW

Before you go, if you enjoyed this book, will you please consider leaving a review on Amazon? As authors, there is nothing we appreciate more than reading reviews on Amazon and other bookseller websites from those who have enjoyed the book.

Thank you so much!
Wendi Blum Weiss & Patricia Wooster